AUDITION MONOLOGS FOR STUDENT ACTORS II

FOR STUDENT ACTORS II

Selections from contemporary plays

EDITED BY
ROGER ELLIS

mp

MERIWETHER PUBLISHING
A division of Pioneer Drama Service, Inc.
Denver, Colorado

Meriwether Publishing
A division of Pioneer Drama Service, Inc.
PO Box 4267
Englewood, CO 80155

www.pioneerdrama.com

Executive editor: Theodore O. Zapel
Cover design: Jan Melvin

The Library of Congress has cataloged the paperback edition as follows:
(Provided by Quality Books, Inc.)

Audition monologs for student actors II : selections from contemporary plays / edited by
    Roger Ellis. -- 1st ed.
        p. cm.
        Includes bibliographical references.
        ISBN 978-1-56608-073-6 (pbk.)
            1. Monologs. 2. Acting--Auditions. I. Ellis, Roger, 1943 May 18-
    PN2080.A886 2001   812'.04508
                                QBI01-201221

Acknowledgments

Among the many individuals who lent me their assistance with this book, special recognition should be given to Grand Valley State University which provided me with the much-needed funding and release time from teaching to compile and prepare the material.

I'm also grateful for the continued support and advice of my editor, Ted Zapel, at Meriwether Publishing Ltd. In addition, I'm indebted to the cooperation of numerous international theatre associations for publicizing my call for scripts. Without the assistance of organizations like AITA/IATA (International Amateur Theatre Association), Women Playwrights International, ASSITEJ/USA (International Association of Youth Theatre), AATE (American Alliance for Theatre in Education), and others, several of the plays included here would not have come to my attention. Credit should also be given to national and international playwrights' associations which publicized my call for scripts, such as La Ronde — the Playwrights' Ring, the American Theatre Web, the International Centre for Women Playwrights, Playwrights on the Web and others. Last but not least I owe a debt of gratitude I can never repay to all of the actors whose performances enabled me to recognize the power and the grace, the subtlety and theatricality of the plays contained in this anthology.

Contents

Introduction

About the Collection

This anthology contains fifty monologs selected from the work of contemporary English-speaking playwrights for young students and actors 10-24 years old. The collection is equally divided between male and female characters, and also contains a variety of pieces for students-of-color. Monologs vary in length from one to two minutes to approximately nine to ten minutes, in order to offer a range of challenges to students for competitive auditions, forensics activities, literary editing, oral interpretation classes, acting studio exercises, and similar applications.

With few exceptions, all of the pieces in this collection are taken from unpublished plays, thus discouraging students from relying upon the already-existing literary or dramatic context of the selections. This intentional limitation seeks to stimulate the student's imaginative resources by urging him or her to supply original background information, given circumstances, character motivation, biographical details and the like for interpreting the texts. A brief introduction precedes each selection in order to highlight some key features and point the student in the right direction. But I hope that the individual speeches — "isolated" from the complete script in this way — will encourage students to "think outside the box" of given plays and stories in order to improvise and discover their own unique interpretations of the material.

In addition to these practical applications for class and studio projects, I believe general readers will also find much to interest them in this collection. For one thing, the book gives voice to nearly forty writers, most of whom are not widely known within the international performance community. I've relied upon writers' organizations, international drama festivals, new plays programs at established theatres, and Internet-based playwrights' organizations in order to publicize my call for scripts. This has succeeded in tapping numerous plays — approximately sixty percent of the collection — which might be regarded either as works-in-progress or local successes deserving wider attention. Both aspects, I believe, signal new work that is up to date, directed at a broad spectrum of contemporary audiences, and generated from a variety of production circumstances.

1

In fact, one of my basic criteria for inclusion is the requirement that all the pieces be taken from plays, and plays that have also been produced in some form: full productions, staged readings, workshops, etc. This is the very best way for writers to develop speakable dialog, compelling character traits, dramatic development and so forth. Unlike the solitary working methods of poets, novelists, and authors in other narrative forms, playwrights need to forge their dramas in the crucible of actor-audience interaction. They need to ensure that their words communicate vividly, vitally and most of all immediately to spectators across the footlights, and score an impact on the audience when spoken. Not all writing, however colorful, functions theatrically in this way; but I feel that all the monologs in this collection are capable of doing so.

A final feature recommending this anthology to teachers, students and general readers is the mildly international flavor of the collection. Approximately one-fifth of these monologs have been written by Canadian or British authors, and this should offer some challenge to students or actors from the United States. For example, is the piece best presented with or without dialect study? And what needs to be researched about the social context or word usage? Also, in almost all cases, the international pieces have historical settings so they require a certain amount of period research in order to unleash their full potential.

Of special concern to me, however, has been the suitability of these monologs for educational purposes. Hence, I've included some brief tips in this introductory section on how to prepare and rehearse the monologs. I've also tried to select only those pieces with characters able to be played by young actors between ten and twenty-four years of age. My hope in doing so has been that the text should serve the special needs of high school and university teachers and students, both as a Drama-in-Education and Theatre for Young Audiences resource. I've also tried to focus on plays containing themes of interest to this age group. Some of the dramas have been specifically written for young audiences such as LISTEN TO OUR VOICES by Claire Braz-Valentine, THE SISTER by Timothy Miller, and VOICES FROM THE SHORE by Max Bush. However, readers will soon discover that the majority of these plays have been written for general audiences, although the monologs contain themes or characters especially appropriate for younger students to examine and develop.

As previously discussed, I've also tried to remain sensitive to considerations of gender and ethnic diversity when making editorial decisions. For example, a number of controversial women writers are included here, as well as female characters both young and old, contemporary and historical. In the category of ethnic diversity, I've sought to include characters from indigenous American, Jewish and other racial or ethnic backgrounds in order to reflect the increasing cultural pluralism both in our schools and in society at large. Also, where necessary, I've indicated gender- and ethnic-specific characters in the acting prefaces to the various selections. Although some of the socially-concerned writers included in this text are often accused of introducing problematic and explosive treatments of gender or racial issues, I've tried to keep the anthology free of vulgar language and strictly adult situations, while still retaining the playwright's incisive treatment of the subject at hand.

I've performed little or no modification of any of the pieces, except to remove them from the context of the entire play and to preface each with brief suggestions on performance approaches. All the monologs have been reviewed and approved by the authors. One of the collection's most interesting features, however, is the variety in length of the selections, because longer monologs offer teachers the opportunity to discuss editing methods with their students. Coaches and students preparing for competitive auditions — scholarships, casting, forensics competitions, etc. — might therefore find value in learning how to trim and focus their selections to a shorter length. On the other hand, I should remind readers that the **printed** length of a monolog is never a good indication of its **performance** length, which always depends on the number of heartbeats — not the number of words. The monologs should therefore be read aloud if only to judge their length, and the emotional power they contain.

For the Coach or Student Preparing Monologs

The first step in working on your monologs is to paraphrase the selection. A paraphrase is a rewording of the original text in your own language — your everyday idioms, speech patterns, word choice, etc. — in order to capture a sense of what is actually being said, and to identify how and why the character's rhetoric differs from yours. The literal meaning of what is being said is the "denotation," and you should always refer to a dictionary when encountering words that seem unfamiliar to you. The **implied** or **underlying** meaning is even more important for your interpretation, and this is called the "connotation." The connotation yields vital clues about the way characters really think and feel, the "subtext" of the monolog. Paraphrasing also highlights the difference between your personality and the dramatic role. Finally, a paraphrase will always alert you about words or phrases you may not have completely understood at first reading.

A second benefit of the paraphrase is that it will help you to personalize the selection. This means that you must find common ground between you and the character you intend to present — both in the favorable as well as unfavorable aspects of that character. By and large, the monologs contained here were selected because they voice one or more concerns that are often commonly shared by young students; so you shouldn't have to reach too far in order to understand and appreciate what is being thought and said. The challenge, however, lies in your ability to also relate to aspects of personality, feelings or values that you **don't** share with the character, or that you reject in your own personal life. In short, in order to fully exploit the monolog's potential you must find some point of contact with **all** the issues, emotions and values that you (the character) will struggle with and express to your audience.

Paraphrasing is a very important first step, and many students ignore writing it out and comparing it with the original because they assume they understand the piece, and of course they're eager to act it out. Remember, though, that you simply cannot effectively present what you don't understand or what you regard as unimportant, objectionable, or embarrassing to present in public. You'll merely be reducing a different and rich dramatic character to your own everyday personality, or worse, going through the motions and mouthing the words. Your performance will ring hollow because the text will signal more than you are able to give it.

After tearing apart the monolog with paraphrase in order to see what's actually contained in it, *your next step is to identify the relationships that the monolog defines.* Bear in mind that every bit of acting you will ever do is based upon relationship — not glorious language or spectacular effects or high-energy emotions or anything else. If you fail to create a relationship with another person when you present your monolog, your performance will seem flat and uninteresting to listeners. We don't come to the theatre or motion pictures to look at the scenery or listen to the music or get blown away by raging passions and clever effects: We come to identify with the people in the story and the problems they grapple with, and hopefully be moved somehow by that experience.

There are two relationships you must always define for yourself: your

4

relationship with the audience or listeners, and your character's relationship with the vis-à-vis. (A "vis-à-vis" is an acting term that means the other imaginary character to whom you're speaking.) In the first case, you must ask yourself why are these ideas important to communicate? What's in it for the audience? How are they supposed to be moved by these words? What should they feel or experience? And how can I accomplish that?

All acting is communication — a point that most people forget because plays and films and television are often regarded merely as entertainment. Actors tend to forget this, too, in the wake of rehearsing, getting onstage, calming their nerves, performing their scenes, and getting through the show. But you must be personally confident that there is something of value in the monolog if you're to do it well. To take someone's mind off their terrible grief for a few moments? To remind them of the common spark of humanity that we all — including villains — share together? To throw some new emphasis on the sufferings of rejected lovers? the fear of loneliness? the sadness of isolation? the numbness of alienation? What exactly is important for you to express to your public in this monolog? There must have been something or you wouldn't have been attracted to it, right?

If you believe this, if you believe in what you need to accomplish with your interpretation, it will be so much easier for you to perform it compellingly, and you'll be much more confident about overcoming the stage fright and jitters that always accompany public presentations. If nothing else, remember that people don't come to the theatre or to films to see ordinary life or experience common emotions. We pay good money to be moved and to get something we just can't find in our everyday lives. So find out what that something is that your monolog can do for the listener, and go for it.

The second relationship you need to clearly define for yourself and the audience is your relationship with the vis-à-vis. You should begin by assuming that you (the character) would die if you could not speak the speech to this particular person, at this particular time. You must assume that you have an itch that you've just got to scratch, a problem that you absolutely must resolve — here and now — with this monolog and with this other person who is listening. Again, remember that nothing in the theatre is ordinary: your relationship to your vis-à-vis must be compelling. Only this person can give you what you need, and this person must give it to you now. You need to believe in this commitment as fully as possible in order to "raise the stakes" and generate the energy that the dramatic situation requires. After all, if you don't believe the speech is important enough for your vis-à-vis to listen to, then we certainly won't listen either.

In some of the monologs you'll find the vis-à-vis clearly defined for you: a lover, a brother, a parent, someone concrete. In most of them, however, you must invent the vis-à-vis for yourself. This is one of the most enjoyable challenges an actor will face, because it allows you to choose any imaginary listener you want for the monolog. In either case — whether the vis-à-vis is defined or not — you should try to imagine that listener as concretely and vividly as possible. Choose details and people from your personal life who will "give" you the most vivid feedback: someone who argues relentlessly with you, someone who throws himself or herself passionately into your arms, abuses you, cheers you on, frustrates you with questions — in short, someone who **disturbs** you as you deliver the speech or tell the story. The more you believe in your imaginary vis-à-vis, the more you will energize your presentation, and the less stage fright will assail you.

When rehearsing the piece, in fact, you should visualize that imaginary listener's actual physical responses to what you're saying in order to strengthen your attempt to clarify, emphasize, persuade and win them over with the speech. Is that listener objecting? about to interrupt? starting to leave and reject what you're saying? laughing at your words? crying at what you're saying? What, exactly? Play with these imaginary responses as you prepare your monolog and use the words of the speech to overcome the objections of your vis-à-vis and get what you want. Fight to communicate and be understood and you will discover your performance taking on a whole new energy, a whole new life the more you succeed with creating this living, breathing, reacting vis-à-vis that we cannot see. If you succeed, we **will** see that character — you'll compel us to do so.

In addition to making the vis-à-vis as concrete and active as possible in this way, you also need to *identify what it is exactly that you're fighting for in the scene.* Here too, the monolog may not exactly tell you what it is you want from the other character, and you will have to invent it. But whether or not your goal is identified by the playwright, you should make it as detailed and as specific as possible in order to play it effectively in the scene. Actors sometimes refer to this as the "goals," "objectives," or "intentions" in the scene, but I prefer to use the verb "fighting for" because it reminds you that you absolutely must struggle to achieve it.

First of all, when beginning to determine what your character is fighting for, remember that in real life no one simply hands us whatever we want. We must demand strongly, insistently, forcefully in order to get what's really important for us in our lives. It is this "fighting for" that lends urgency and especially sharp focus to your acting. Combined with a concrete vis-à-vis, this active goal for your speech will add up to a performance that is rich with energy and loaded with interest for your listeners.

Secondly, take a tip from professional actors who often identify this "fighting for" in terms of a strong, active, infinitive verb. You want **to guilt** him in the monolog, **to mock** her, **to drive** him to tears, **to seduce** her kind feelings, **to demand** he apologize, **to trick** her out of money, **to fall desperately** in love with you, and so forth. Again, many beginning actors overlook this important step of choosing concrete actions to play in the scene, feeling that their "instincts" and the words alone will "carry them through" the performance. This can be the kiss of death for a student because when you've failed to highlight the specific reasons, moment-by-moment, for which you're speaking, then you're going to miss a lot of the emotional colors, the changing thought patterns, the shifts in mood and changes in tactics that add shape and importance to your enactment.

Of course, real life also tells us that what we want from other people is rarely single-minded or simple. Our goals, our "fighting fors" are often multiple and can be very complex. So, too, in the monologs which follow, be aware that the character's objectives will change and develop as he or she continues speaking. No single "fighting for" will get you through the entire speech. This means that in every monolog you must "end up" in a different emotional or spiritual place than where you began. Something **must** happen in the course of the speech, some change **must** occur.

This brings us to the next step you must perform: *eventing the script*. The great American acting teacher Michael Shurtleff was fond of using this phrase. What it means is that you must divide the monolog into a beginning, a middle, and an end; and that you must find in each of those the sub-sections or "beats" where "events" — physical or psychological — happen to you. Where do your thoughts change? Where do your verbal tactics change? Have you discovered something new as you speak? Do the stage directions indicate that you physically do some things at certain points? Does that lead you into new directions? And how does all this add up to the final point you want to reach in the monolog? In short, what is the **pattern of actions** in the monolog that takes you from point A to point Z? Another great American acting teacher, Uta Hagen, once remarked that the pattern of actions you choose to play in your monolog or scene is the single most effective thing you can do to improve your acting.

When you rehearse your monolog, you must strive to play each of these beats separately and distinctly in order to "mark" the progress or development of your thoughts in the piece. If you do this, you'll find sudden **contrasts** where one beat changes to another as the result of some new idea. You'll stumble upon those highly dramatic moments of **discovery** as you speak. You'll also make surprising **connections and transitions** from one idea or emotional state to another. And the **pace** of your delivery and **emotional moods** will vary, propelling the monolog forward and engaging your listeners' attention moment-by-moment as you act it out.

As you read the prefatory remarks I've supplied before each of the selections in this book, you'll notice that I frequently use the terms "ladder" or "stepping-stone" to identify the kind of structure the piece displays. These are handy terms for actors. They refer broadly to the shape of events as the writer has constructed them. In a ladder-type of speech, the events and the intensity build more or less consistently from beginning to end where the point of maximum dramatic tension occurs. By contrast, in a stepping-stone monolog — and always in the longer, "extended" monologs — you're likely to find a **series** of dramatic peaks throughout the speech, before it eventually reaches its major climax at or near the end.

Whichever structure seems to govern the monolog, however, it will be up to you to identify all those steps — those beats — along the way, and to play each distinctly as part of a pattern. Never end a monolog at the same emotional or spiritual place that you began. Play the selection so that important events happen to the character en route, in order to make us believe that his or her world has changed dramatically by the time the speech is finished.

Rehearsing Monologs

Once you've completed the preparatory work discussed above, you're ready to rehearse. Your first step in rehearsal is to *score your script*. This means marking-up your script, treating it as a musical "score" that you'll use in performance. You'll need at least three copies for this: two "rough drafts" and a "final" version. When you get copies, try to get them larger than the printed text you ordinarily find in published playscripts; and always mark your script in pencil because you're going to change your mind often as rehearsals proceed.

Actors use a variety of notations to score their scripts. Probably the most familiar is the use of highlighter pens to identify words or phrases you want to **vocally emphasize**. But there are other things besides emphasis that are important to you. For one thing, you should always draw a line across the page to **separate the beats** in a monolog and reinforce their distinctness in your mind as you memorize and rehearse. And penciled notations in the margin beside each beat keep you focused on the infinitive phrase that tells you **what you're fighting for** there. Actors also frequently draw a diagonal line between words, phrases or sentences to indicate **where pauses should occur**. An asterisk or a circled word connected by a line to a margin note can remind you of **physical actions or staging movements** that should occur at that point. Some other marginal notations I like to make in scripts include wavy lines that suggest **changes in tempo or pace**, or small arrows indicating rising or falling **inflections in vocal delivery**.

Don't overdo this, of course, because you won't be following every mark on the page when you eventually go onstage. But physically scoring the script in this way helps you to identify and set the technical aspects of the monolog in your mind prior to memorizing it. It also helps you to exploit all the literary and dramatic aspects of the writing the author has given you. You'll be surprised what you turn up. And of course, if you're doing a non-memorized oral interpretation of the monolog, then you'll want to gradually reduce the notations to just those that you find are absolutely essential, and that you can comfortably and effectively follow as you read it publicly.

Next you must *memorize the monolog, or key sections of it, for an effective presentation.* Of course, for a theatrical audition and many class assignments the piece must be entirely memorized. Only when you free yourself from reading the text off a page, and instead can speak it confidently and naturally, will you be able to identify psycho-physically with the character. Even with non-memorized presentations, as with any public address, you should always memorize the key sections that require maximum eye contact, maximum emotional intensity, maximum belief in and commitment to the dramatic situation. Memorization also frees you to physicalize the actions in the text with hand and arm gestures, blocking movements in the space, and changes in posture and body position.

Allow yourself plenty of time for staged rehearsals, and these should serve several purposes. For one thing, get used to the sound of your voice, and work to connect voice and movement in order to gain a "natural" feel for living the life of the character. Also you must always rehearse the monolog aloud. Running it over in your head again and again will do absolutely nothing for you, and only serve to increase your nervousness and insecurity. Most of all, however, avoid treating the rehearsal as an attempt to finally "get it memorized" — to get it all set and fixed and consistent. Instead, use much of your rehearsal time to discover new things to do in the monolog, both vocally and physically.

Remember that there will be plenty of time later on to drill yourself for sheer memorization and repeatability, and to keep it fresh and spontaneous. You can just bet that you'll be speaking it aloud to yourself in the shower, in the car, while you're "waiting in the wings" or whatever. People will likely think you're going crazy talking to yourself so much. So always use rehearsals to uncover new possibilities you may have overlooked, to exploit each and every phrase for maximum dramatic potential, and to "open up" the text by experimenting with surprising and original choices for physical actions and vocal power.

One aspect of rehearsals that seems to consistently trouble young actors is the question of physical movement or blocking that a monolog may require. In general, young actors tend to make **too many** movements — random paces and crosses, or nervous hand and arm gestures — that only serve to muddy the dramatic action taking place or to confuse the spectator. Rehearsals are often valuable, therefore, for **reducing** the movements that may have cluttered the enactment. Remember that movements should **only** underscore what is happening in the text; never move just for the sake of moving, or because you feel you've been standing in one place for too long. What matters are the heartbeats expressed in the monolog, not how much visual variety and excitement you're giving the onlookers.

To devise effective movements for yourself, you should begin with the stage directions offered by the playwright. While it's not essential for you to perform them, they certainly do give a good indication of where the monolog **might** be enhanced by a certain kind of gesture or posture or movement. Next, you want to be certain to place your imaginary vis-a-vis downstage of you so that you can be fully visible from the front where the listeners will see you. You can then seek to physicalize (emphasize and set-off) each beat of the monolog by changing your stage position in relation to your vis-à-vis: circling him or her, approaching or withdrawing, turning away, threatening, pleading, etc. Some of the monologs even contain sections where characters speak directly "out" (into the auditorium), such as at moments of reflection or recollection. At these points you can move downstage to do just that — although never look straight at a director or auditor or forensics judge in a competitive performance situation.

One type of movement, however, that you should always avoid is pantomiming of objects such as furniture or hand properties. This always "breaks the illusion" you're seeking to create and reminds the audience that you're "acting." Limit yourself to a simple table and a couple of chairs, and devise ways to do without any other props or furniture that you might be tempted to add, or that seem indicated in the text. I've tried to be careful in selecting monologs for this book, and there are none that absolutely **require** any physical objects for their presentation. On the other hand, a small physical prop can be very reassuring in the actor's hand when it comes to mastering stage fright. For example, a book or magazine or eyeglasses — particularly when it's suggested in the script or can be made to seem natural and appropriate in the situation — might sometimes help the presentation. But in most cases, hand properties — like costumes or special furniture — are unnecessary. What the spectators want to see is you, not the furniture.

You can also help yourself in the rehearsal process by finding people to listen to you once you've shaped the piece into a presentable form. Friends are always good for this because they give you a chance to accustom yourself to eyeballs actually **looking** at you while you perform it. They can also spot obvious mannerisms you may have overlooked because you're so close to the material and you've been rehearsing it so much. For example, are you unconsciously using the same hand gestures over and over again? (Have them plug their ears and just watch you.) Or does your voice fall into repetitious vocal patterns the longer you continue? (Have them close their eyes and just listen to you.) Friends can also pass along some ideas that you might not have considered: possibilities for movement or different interpretations of lines or phrases.

A second valuable type of live spectator is a teacher or director who can coach you as a critical listener. This is absolutely essential with competitive auditions of any kind. A dramatic coach will be more objective than your friends in assessing whether or not the enactment "shows you at your best," or in suggesting where you need to push yourself more to derive the maximum dramatic value from a phrase or

11

section of the speech. Finally, dramatic coaches are valuable critics for all those "technical" things that tend to escape us when we self-rehearse. Are you projecting well at all points in the monolog? Are you exceeding the time limits? Can **every word** be heard? Do the movements enhance or muddy the sense of the speech? Are you looking at the floor sometimes as you act? Is the pacing monotonous, are the transitions sharp, and are the emotional colors expressed with sufficient variety?

I hope that all these suggestions will help you in preparing the monologs that follow, and perhaps you have other helpful techniques of your own that I haven't covered here. Remember that dramatic literature is not something that can be completely apprehended at a single sitting like a movie, TV show or E-mail. It's designed to be acted, to be rehearsed and explored again and again, and to be shaped — to be fleshed-out by the unique, original choices that each and every actor may bring to it. Don't concentrate so much on "getting it right" because there is no one "right" way to do it, any more than there is only one "right" Hamlet or one "right" Ophelia. Hamlet and Ophelia are only the actors presently playing the roles, with their own singularities, original choices, emotional responses and personal interpretations. Be brave, take risks, and make **your** own original choices that will enliven the selections that follow.

A Reminder About Intellectual Property

In all the anthologies I edit, I feel compelled to remind readers that the monologs in the collection are intended **only** for studio exercises or for reading. When it comes to performing them, producing them in public readings, or adapting them in any way via the electronic media for other audiences — educational, amateur, or professional — then permission **must** be obtained and royalties paid to the agent or author.

Perhaps this "caution" needs to be restated in this age of the Internet where so much is available online or otherwise reproducible at little or no charge. Readers must remind themselves that plays — like other unique, cultural artifacts — are not equivalent to the bytes and "factoids" we slug through and manipulate by the thousands every day. They are the intellectual property of human beings who have spent many years earning, and who therefore deserve, proper acknowledgment and compensation for producing and distributing them to the public.

Bear in mind that I'm attempting in this book to highlight and promote the work of a handful of uniquely talented and very highly motivated artists whose worth, importance and cultural value in our society is already deeply discounted, frequently ridiculed, and even despised. Their plays are their honest work, their "products." Pay for them. If you wish to perform any of these monologs in public, credits appear at the end of this volume; call or write for permission. These artists are not unreasonable in what they expect from us.

MONOLOGS FOR WOMEN

Grace Notes
by Rachel Rubin Ladutke

1 Catherine — 19   Female — Serious

2

3 *(Catherine recently gave up her baby for adoption. She is*
4 *speaking to her 16-year-old sister Emily. It is 1967. They are in*
5 *the kitchen of their farmhouse in Connecticut. The actor should*
6 *avoid falling into the "trap" of reminiscence and nostalgia in*
7 *presenting this piece, and remember that even in recalling the*
8 *sad memories, Catherine is struggling to overcome the*
9 *wrenching feelings of guilt and grief about giving her baby up*
10 *for adoption. She is not dreamily recalling an event somewhere*
11 *in her past: she is desperately "scratching this itch" over and*
12 *over again. This is a powerful piece that moves through several*
13 *small climaxes, discoveries and surprises, until it reaches a*
14 *final climax in the last few lines.)*

15

16 Every time I get to sleep, I keep having the same dream.
17 I'm walking through this long hallway, and there's
18 nobody else around. Except, I'm walking a little dog. It's
19 really friendly and it loves me. All of a sudden this door
20 opens — I didn't even see it. It's at the end of the hall,
21 right in front of me. There's a really bright light, and
22 voices, and I start feeling faint. The next thing I know, I
23 wake up and the dog is gone. Just when I open my eyes,
24 I hear the door slam shut. As soon as I feel like I can
25 get up, I turn the knob, but it won't open. I try and try,
26 but the door's locked tight. I start crying and screaming,
27 and then I see a window and I notice it's snowing out.
28 So I go outside, and I start dancing in the snow. I feel
29 so free, I can almost forget about losing the dog. Off in

1   the distance I see a little building, and I start running
2   towards it. When I get close enough, I see that it's an
3   animal shelter, and I realize what I really want is to get
4   another dog. But the woman in the shelter says I can't.
5   Somehow she knows I felt happy when the dog
6   disappeared, and she tells me I don't deserve another
7   one. I beg and beg her, and finally she agrees to let me
8   look at their dogs. But I can't find any like the one I lost,
9   and that's the only one I want. I start crying. Then I wake
10   up, and I'm really crying. I don't remember much about
11   giving birth, but I know I heard her cry. I didn't get to
12   look at her, or hold her. The nurse even said I didn't
13   deserve to see her, because I was giving her away. They
14   did let me feed her once. I had to refuse to sign the
15   papers before they'd even let me do that. She had blue
16   eyes. I think most babies have blue eyes, but hers
17   weren't at all pale. They were really deep, deep blue. Like
18   the ocean. One hour, that's all we had together. Then
19   they took her away again. You know what I really don't
20   get, Emmy? When I talked to the other girls at the
21   agency, they all kept saying they couldn't wait to give
22   birth so they could get back to normal. But I didn't want
23   to have the baby, because then I was going to lose her.
24   I tried to keep her with me as long as I could. I started
25   having pains in the middle of the night, but I didn't wake
26   Mom up until I couldn't stand it any more. I didn't want
27   to go to the hospital, 'cause I knew I'd be coming home
28   alone and empty. That's the worst part, I think. I feel so
29   empty. I'm cold all the time. And now everyone expects
30   me to just go on like nothing happened. They lied to me.
31   Nobody told me it would be like this. I'm not even twenty
32   years old, Emily, and I feel like my life is over. And I just
33   keep waiting for it to stop hurting. But it doesn't. It just
34   gets worse. You don't know how much it hurts. *(Pause.)*
35   Emmy. Hold me?

Voices from the Shore
by Max Bush

1   Beth — 17   Female — Serious

2

3   *(Beth is desperately trying to patch things up with her*
4   *boyfriend who has meant more to her over the years than*
5   *"ordinary" boyfriends ever could. Unfortunately, she's also*
6   *very dependent upon him, and that makes the following*
7   *impassioned speech not only desperate but also somehow*
8   *threatening — she's very vulnerable at this moment. The*
9   *monolog is climactic in its form, and it requires that the actor*
10 *visualize a "Joel" to herself as concretely as possible, all the*
11 *way through, as she pleads with him.)*

12

13 When I first started liking you, there were a lot of
14 opposing forces — such as my past reputation. But still
15 I wanted to see you. So I started to try and dress better
16 and clean up my act for what seemed like the fifty
17 billionth time, but somehow I knew that this time it
18 would work. Instead of "Gimme drugs! Gimme drugs!"
19 I'm saying "Gimme Joel! Gimme Joel!" And then, when
20 I went three weeks without bring grounded for life, again,
21 my parents even liked you. *(Pause.)* And then you, you
22 made this dream with me, about college and getting
23 married and a family. I hadn't thought about that
24 before — not really, not for me. It's taken me about four
25 years to go through the garbage to finally find a person
26 like you, and if we break up now, I'm afraid I'll go back
27 to what I was. But I can't do this by myself; you HAVE
28 to talk to me. Because — because Freebe's calling,
29 again, and I didn't know what was wrong with us, I

19

1   almost went out with him last night — you have to stop
2   me, Joel, or I'll just go. I will. I'll just go.
3
4
5
6
7
8
9
10
11
12
13
14
15
16
17
18
19
20
21
22
23
24
25
26
27
28
29
30
31
32
33
34
35

Waving Goodbye
by Jamie Pachino

1	Lily — 17	Female — Serious

2

3   *(Lily Blue is a photographer who has lost her father in a*
4   *mountain climbing accident, and must spend her seventeenth*
5   *year with the mother who abandoned her. The playwright*
6   *tells us the play "is about loss, grief, change, making art,*
7   *being stalled, wishing things were different, moving forward,*
8   *first love, not turning into your mother, and those irrevocable*
9   *moments where nothing is ever the same." The actor's*
10   *challenge in this monolog is to discover how the piece can*
11   *express as many of those emotional colors as possible. Lily is*
12   *speaking to Boggy, her new boyfriend; and "my favorite*
13   *thing she ever did" refers to a piece of sculpture that her*
14   *artist-mother created and that has shattered in a fight she just*
15   *had with her mom.)*

16

17   **Boggy, sometimes I dream my father falls, and I can**
18   **catch him. I race and I grope until I'm standing right**
19   **under him, with my arms open wide. But instead his**
20   **weight crushes me, and we fall to the ground, and**
21   **nobody survives. Sometimes my father dies because I'm**
22   **too insignificant to break his fall.** *(Enormously hurt:)* **That**
23   **was my favorite thing she ever did. I was ten when I saw**
24   **it the first time. She had gone off to ... the Serengeti, I**
25   **think. The month of March is supposed to be, I don't**
26   **know — she has this thing about light and water and ...**
27   **she'd gone off before, but this time we were pretty sure**
28   **she wasn't coming back. And he had to go off on a**
29   **climb. The hot water heater was busted, the mortgage**

1   was overdue, Pepper our dog — needed an operation,
2   and he had to leave. So he took me to this locker where
3   she kept her early stuff, because he wanted me to know
4   something about her. To understand why she was right,
5   he said, to go away when the world asked her to,
6   because of what the world got back. Not me, not him,
7   just ... the world. But there aren't so many ways to say
8   that to a ten year-old, so he took me to see her work. I
9   didn't know anything about art, but something about the
10 forearms and the hands ... my father's hands that she
11 had done ... And he showed me all the work she'd done
12 right after they met, and told me how she ate Hershey
13 bars at 12,000 feet after climbing without any of the
14 right equipment, and how it was a miracle she didn't die
15 right there. He smiled so big when he told how those first
16 pieces made her name, how her vision of him had made
17 her — who she turned into — even though she had
18 grown past them and wouldn't look at them any more.
19 Even though they were his favorites, and my favorites,
20 she had to go off hunting new light. They were so
21 incredible, I almost forgave her.
22
23
24
25
26
27
28
29
30
31
32
33
34
35

"A Genius," from *Fun House Mirror*
by Dori Appel

1 Jill — 18+	Female — Serious

2

3 *(Jill is telling her big sister, Amelia, how she used to feel as*
4 *a child when Amelia failed to take care of her — as agreed —*
5 *in their mother's absence. This is an excellent example of a*
6 *simple ladder speech, where the character gradually becomes*
7 *more tense and finds it increasingly more difficult to speak as*
8 *she relates the painful incident from her past life. Many young*
9 *actors can certainly relate to this common experience. The*
10 *monolog culminates in a powerful moment of revelation that*
11 *says as much about Jill's present insecurities as it does about*
12 *her past sufferings.)*

13

14 Here we are, six years old and ten, and it's starting to
15 get dark. A little while ago you slipped off to Mother's
16 room and locked the door, and now I'm starting to get
17 scared. "Amelia?" I call, but there isn't any answer.
18 "Amelia?" I knock on the door, and listen. There isn't a
19 sound. Did something in there get you? Is it going to
20 come out and get me? I'm trying not to cry — if I cry,
21 I'm afraid something awful will happen to me. So I force
22 myself — FORCE myself — to walk away from that
23 door. I go to the wicker chest where we keep our toys,
24 and I take out my coloring book or paper dolls and the
25 cardboard candy box that holds my crayons and
26 scissors. All the time I'm saying to myself, "Don't be
27 scared, don't be scared, don't be scared." Then I lay my
28 things down on the table very carefully — without
29 disturbing the salt and pepper shakers or the pad of

1   paper that Mother uses for grocery lists — and I tell
2   myself that if I cut all the doll clothes out exactly right,
3   I'll be safe. I sit alone at the table for what seems like
4   forever, cutting and cutting with my round, blunt
5   scissors, and dressing all the flat, smiling paper dolls in
6   their jaunty clothes. Then at last — oh, at LAST! —
7   Mother comes home, and you appear from somewhere,
8   and she cooks supper, and we sit down together and eat.
9   Amelia ... *(SHE breaks down.)* ... I'm still coloring
10 perfectly and cutting out everything just right, and it
11 doesn't help! It doesn't make anything safe!
12
13
14
15
16
17
18
19
20
21
22
23
24
25
26
27
28
29
30
31
32
33
34
35

An Odious Damned Lie
by Lewis W. Heniford

1	Loris — 16

Female — Serious

1   Loris — 16   Female — Serious

2

3   *(Loris is speaking to her boyfriend Mike about her intention*

4   *to leave home. Mike has just protested her decision, but she*

5   *then shows him the bruises of her mother's latest beating, and*

6   *he is shocked. The following speech explains her decision to*

7   *him, but it is also the first outpouring that Loris has ever*

8   *made to anyone about the suffering her mother has caused*

9   *her over the years. The monolog contains two climactic*

10 *points, one in the middle and the other towards the end.)*

11

12 Last night. I was in my room, going over the scene. She

13 came in, sat on my bed, and watched. I tried to do it the

14 best I could, to impress her, to get her to understand

15 how much this means to me. She started tapping her

16 glass against the foot of the bed, but I stayed in

17 character. Part of me was wondering about her reaction,

18 still I went on. When it was over, she looked at me, she

19 took another drink, then just sat there looking at me. I

20 waited, sitting at my desk. Then she started laughing.

21 She came over to me and started punching me. It was

22 light at first, you know, just taps. Then it got harder.

23 Suddenly she stopped and started to leave the room.

24 She stumbled and had to catch on to the door handle to

25 keep from falling. Then she started crying, laughing and

26 crying. She stopped, grew quiet. Just stared at me. She

27 went over to the frame where I used to have your

28 picture. It was just the frame, nothing in it. She wanted

29 to know where the picture is. I told her I'd thrown it out,

1   as she'd told me to do. She didn't believe me. She knew
2   I was lying. She came at me with the glass, hitting me
3   with it. She was screaming and got louder and louder. I
4   kept thinking they would hear her next door. I had been
5   backing away, but when she got so loud, I did
6   something. I ducked under her arm. You know how they
7   teach us in swimming to get to the rear of someone who
8   is panicking? It was like I was in the water and she was
9   drowning. I got behind her and grabbed one of her arms,
10 bent it around behind her with one hand, then I put my
11 other arm around her neck. I started to pull her, I don't
12 know where I was trying to pull her. But my arm started
13 getting tighter and tighter around her neck. I pulled and
14 pulled and held her tighter and tighter. She collapsed.
15 She was just limp, and my arm was holding her ...
16 tighter. I was trying to save her. I was trying to kill her.
17 I don't know. I don't know what I was trying to do. I
18 somehow got her on to my bed. She just lay there. You
19 know, she was all limp, but in her hand was the glass.
20 She may have been dying, but she had enough strength
21 to hold on to that glass. I pried it from her fingers and
22 put it on the nightstand. I didn't know what to do next.
23 I thought about phoning for an ambulance. I thought
24 about calling you. I just sat beside her and took her into
25 my arms and started crying. Then I could feel her coming
26 back. It was faint, then stronger, then I knew she was
27 going to live. She began to cough. I got the glass, ran
28 into the bathroom and got some water, and brought it to
29 her. I helped her sip. She kept looking at me as she took
30 little sips, at first, then more. She finished the glass and
31 spoke. She said, "Get me a drink." I started to the
32 bathroom with the glass, but she said, "I mean a drink."
33 She kept staring at me. I went into her room and poured
34 whisky into the glass and brought it to her. She kept
35 staring, and smiled, and said, "Thanks, I owe you." I felt

1   I feared her. She always used to say that before she beat
2   me. There was something in the way she said it; she
3   really meant it. I almost knew what was going to happen
4   next. I sat on the edge of the bed and waited. She
5   finished her drink slowly as if using it to bring back all
6   her strength; I waited for my mother to beat me, again.
7   And she did. With the glass, after she'd emptied it. As
8   she hit me I thought the glass might break and cut me
9   and even kill me. I hoped she wouldn't kill me. But I let
10   her hit. I cried out for mercy, and I let her hit and hit and
11   hit. I let her. I kept thinking, this is it, this is the last
12   time you will ever beat me, so go ahead and make the
13   most of it. She hit me until she was tired. We were both
14   on the floor. Then she got up and stumbled out of the
15   room. She wasn't laughing or crying any more. She was
16   just gasping for breath. I heard her go to her room and
17   slam the door. I locked my door and took off my clothes
18   and looked in the mirror. Somehow, as always, she'd
19   been careful to hit me only where it wouldn't show,
20   where my clothes would cover the bruises. I got into the
21   shower and let the water run cold over the marks, to
22   keep them from swelling. I just let it run and run. That's
23   what I always did when she beat me. But this time, I
24   knew it was the last time ... I'm leaving home.
25
26
27
28
29
30
31
32
33
34
35

Playground
by Sybil M. Odom, Ph.D.

1	Susie — 13	Female — Comic

2

3   *(Susie begins this piece reading from a diary that belongs to*

4   *her older sister: She's in detention after school, musing to*

5   *herself and trying to make the time pass. The monolog is*

6   *unique in that it permits the actor to play a genuine sense of*

7   *"spontaneity" in performance: time passes, and the actor-*

8   *character must improvise something to amuse herself — and*

9   *the auditors — until her detention is over. Of course, the*

10   *monolog isn't improvised at all, but that's the acting*

11   *challenge here — to play the character so believably that the*

12   *words seem to pop right out spontaneously. The key to doing*

13   *that is to let the emotions overcome you as you encounter*

14   *them: mystery, surprise, shock, impatience — to mention but*

15   *a few.)*

16

17   **Dear diary ... he KISSED ME! What was it like? Well, it**

18   **was kinda like riding a roller coaster. I felt dizzy and**

19   **alive ... and then I felt like I was gonna throw up. They**

20   **never tell you that part in the romance novels — the**

21   **woofing your cookies part.** *(SHE puts the diary down.)*

22   **Ugh! I think I'm going to throw up. My sister, Alex, she**

23   **likes to write** *(Indicating the diary:).* **Isn't it romantic? I**

24   **bet she's home right now dreaming dreams of**

25   **unrequited love. I put oatmeal in her shoes.** *(SHE offers*

26   *the audience her lollipop.)* **Want a lick?** *(Pulls the lollipop*

27   *back.)* **PSYCH! If you could have lunch with anyone in**

28   **the world — what would you order? Me, I'm still at**

29   **school. Detention. I know it looks as if I threw butter on**

1   the wall but in actuality I'm in Home Ec conducting a
2   time continuum experiment in metaphysics. Then out of
3   nowhere — WHAM! — I'm in detention! I'm severely
4   under-appreciated at this school. What if the Hokey
5   Pokey really IS what it's all about? Check it out. This is
6   my control group. *(SHE gestures into the audience towards*
7   *an imaginary wall.)* On the right, butter. On the left, I
8   Can't Believe It's Not Butter. I'm waiting to see which
9   one will slide down the wall first. I can't stand my
10   Home Ec teacher. No, really. *(Confidentially:)* She eats
11   our homework. HEY! There goes the margarine! Man
12   your posts. *(SUZIE checks her watch.)* Going, going,
13   GONE! Seventy-two minutes and forty-eight seconds!
14   AWESOME! Why do they call it rush hour when nothing
15   moves? Think about it. Now stop. You think I'm a brat,
16   don't you? I'm not really. It's all an elaborate ruse. You
17   see, people role-play, and if I'm the bad child, then my
18   sister gets to be the good child. So really I'm just trying
19   to help Alex. That's me: always thinking of others. And
20   besides ... it's FUN! Who was Casper the Friendly Ghost
21   before he died? He looks suspiciously like Richie Rich to
22   me. *(Long pause.)* You know, I don't think the butter's
23   coming down.
24
25
26
27
28
29
30
31
32
33
34
35

Fishing the Moon
by Scott McMorrow

1 Young Woman — teens	Female — Serious

3   *(This is a climactic speech, with the peak of emotional*
4   *intensity occurring close to the very end. It is somewhat*
5   *unusual, however, because the Young Woman's tale is*
6   *strongly colored by her recollection of the incident and her*
7   *emotional need to distance herself from the painful emotions*
8   *by dampening the experience in recounting it. The actor must*
9   *therefore be careful to avoid delivering the speech as a*
10   *"memory piece," containing little emotional involvement in*
11   *the narration. A second interesting feature for the actor to play*
12   *is the Young Woman's repeated attempts to avoid discussing*
13   *the incident by seizing upon any occasion to "parade her*
14   *knowledge" of sea conditions, the emergency drill followed*
15   *by the crew, the "funny thing" of how boats behave in the*
16   *waves, etc. The piece becomes most engaging when the*
17   *auditors can sense the powerful fear underlying the Young*
18   *Woman's story.)*

20   **The storm hit in the blackness of night. Wind and waves**
21   **roaring and slamming the boat like a wild beast. All I**
22   **could do was turn the bow straight into the worst of it.**
23   **We didn't want to take one broadside. They say you can**
24   **tell where you are in a wave by the color of the thing.**
25   **Clear and foamy puts you near the top. When you look**
26   **out the wheelhouse and see green then you're**
27   **somewhere in the middle. If you're staring into dark, the**
28   **boat is at the base of the thing and it's most likely time**
29   **to go to Jesus. Course, for us, it was night, now wasn't**

1   it. Tough to tell between green and black. One thing was
2   sure, there was nothing clear in sight.
3   Lost the auto-pilot right off. Had to steer her by
4   hand. The whole crew was up, bouncing around like
5   popcorn. We tied a man, Rick was his name, to the
6   wheel just so he could keep both hands on it. Next thing
7   we knew a monster wave smashed into the forward
8   window and shattered it. Water was pouring in hard and
9   fast. Everyone was in their survival suits. I had the crew
10   get out the saw. The plan was to cut up the galley table
11   and plug the broken window. The ropes we tied around
12   Rick's wrists were cutting into him hard, drawing blood.
13   Poor soul never got time to complain. Another huge
14   wave crested over the bow and nailed him square in the
15   chest. Blew him right through the side of the
16   wheelhouse and into the churning sea. The plan
17   changed in a heartbeat. I had the boys tie themselves
18   together by running a rope around their waists while I
19   turned the boat. Took a couple broadside that almost
20   put us under. We got the spotlight on Rick. He was
21   bobbing up and down like a cork. Each man on deck
22   took up a gaff. I was planning to bring Rick alongside so
23   we could jab the oversized hooks into him. I was yelling
24   not to stick him in any vital organs, just jab him
25   through a shoulder or leg. There they were, lined up on
26   the starboard rail hoping for the chance to impale our
27   crew mate. Funny thing about boats. The V-shape hull
28   means you've got to actually hit the target so it'll run
29   down the side. Rick was about three feet off the bow
30   when a wave rolled the boat. We could all hear him
31   screaming at us as he passed down the opposite side.
32   That was the last we saw of Rick. We still had other fish
33   in the skillet. The ocean was still pouring in through the
34   wheelhouse window. While I kept calling in the May Day
35   the crew formed a bucket brigade to bail the water out.

1   By daybreak the worst of it was over. When the Coast
2   Guard arrived they said it looked like we had been
3   through a war.
4
5
6
7
8
9
10
11
12
13
14
15
16
17
18
19
20
21
22
23
24
25
26
27
28
29
30
31
32
33
34
35

The Belles of the Mill
by Rachel Rubin Ladutke

1   Elizabeth — 21   Female — Serious

2

3   *(This speech is taken from a play recounting the gripping*

4   *story of women mill workers who stage a bold strike in*

5   *Ragtime-era New England, during the bitter winter of 1912.*

6   *The public assembly context of the monolog is evident, and*

7   *the actor must remember to deliver the piece directly to the*

8   *house, with strength, intensity, and careful attention to vocal,*

9   *verbal, and physical resources. In short, this is not a "tame"*

10   *speech, and it should not be attempted by an actor who does*

11   *not feel confident with the defiant energy and inspiring*

12   *rhetoric that the words require. The actor should not feel*

13   *confined to a stationary position – such as an imaginary*

14   *podium or rostrum; but should make full use of the stage as*

15   *in a meeting hall context, "working the crowd" with*

16   *movement and gesture to best advantage. Finally, the actor*

17   *should also note the humor in the speech, as well as the joy*

18   *that underlies the "rabble-rousing" tenor of the challenge that*

19   *Elizabeth Gurley Flynn delivers to her audience.)*

20

21   **Fellow workers! Thank you for coming today! My name**

22   **is Elizabeth Gurley Flynn. I am most proud to be helping**

23   **to lead this strike. I have not worked in the mills myself,**

24   **but I know this life you lead all too well. I spent part of**

25   **my childhood in Manchester, just north of here. There**

26   **have been other strikes here in Lawrence, I know this. I**

27   **None of them had much effect, I know this too. But I**

28   **have seen many strikes in my young life. Marched a few**

29   **times too, you can be sure. And I can tell you that if you**

1   keep your hands in your pockets, you are sure to prevail.
2   The police, the militia, and the National Guard will all
3   fail. They cannot weave cloth with bayonets! They
4   cannot spin wool with clubs! They cannot run looms with
5   rifles! As I walked to this meeting, I was saddened by the
6   sight of children begging in the streets, walking nearly
7   barefoot in the snow, shivering in thin cotton coats. This
8   in a town where good strong cloth is made and sent all
9   over the world! Made by your hands! When you left your
10   homelands, you were promised many things. Joy.
11   Prosperity. Freedom! And tell me, is this what you have
12   found in America? When you boarded those boats, did
13   you realize that you would be herded into mills like
14   animals? That you would be at the mercy of corporations
15   and stockholders for your jobs, your food, your very
16   survival? That you would find closed doors and turned
17   backs everywhere you go? And if you had known this,
18   would you have come so joyously and willingly and
19   expectantly? Of course not. But do not fear. Some day
20   you will all possess what you have earned, which is the
21   right to all the fruits of your labor, and the capitalist mill
22   bosses will have to go begging in the streets. Justice will
23   prevail, and it will be due to your efforts, your strength,
24   and your determination to forge a better life for
25   yourselves and your families. The real enemy is the boss
26   who tries to separate you and keep you hating one
27   another. And the real power is in solidarity.
28   Togetherness. All for one. You are all one family. This is
29   the reason you came to America, and this is what you
30   can still get from America. It has not yet happened, but
31   it can and it must. So let us all join together — skilled
32   and unskilled workers, from all over the globe, men,
33   women, and children. We will emerge victorious! We will
34   sing! We will march! We will unite! *(Sings, to the melody of*
35   *"The Battle Hymn of the Republic":)* **"Solidarity forever,**

1   solidarity forever, solidarity forever ... the union makes
2   us strong!"
3
4
5
6
7
8
9
10
11
12
13
14
15
16
17
18
19
20
21
22
23
24
25
26
27
28
29
30
31
32
33
34
35

I Am Marguerite
by Shirley Barrie

1   Marguerite — 21   Female — Serious

2

3   *(Marguerite, ragged and dirty, has been abandoned on a*

4   *desert island by her brother. She had tried to join him on a*

5   *voyage to the New World in 1542, but her brother discovered*

6   *that she had fallen in love with an unsuitable young*

7   *nobleman aboard ship. Now, abandoned on the island, she is*

8   *on the verge of madness when she sees a fishing boat*

9   *dropping anchor. Her confused mind finds the prospect of*

10   *returning to France more terrifying than another cold winter*

11   *alone in the New World. Torn and struggling between the*

12   *decision to live or to die, she conjures up remembered,*

13   *imagined and possible future encounters with her lover, her*

14   *nurse, her brother, and her mentor, the queen. The monolog*

15   *is extremely challenging because of its "stream of*

16   *consciousness" approach, and because of the movement*

17   *opportunities presented by the stage business it contains. As*

18   *the piece begins, she stumbles onstage holding a fish she has*

19   *just caught.)*

20

21   *(Laughing:)* **You kept me in that stream, my friend, until**

22   **my feet were numb and I thought I would faint from the**

23   **hunger. But now ...** *(SHE sees that the fire has gone out.)*

24   **Holy Mother of**   *(Without success, SHE tries to blow on*

25   *the coals to bring it back to life. She's too hungry. SHE takes*

26   *the fish, slices off a hunk of its flesh and eats it. Slices again.*

27   *A bird trills musically.)* **Eugene? Is that you?** *(SHE throws*

28   *down the fish and the knife guiltily, and runs to get the lute*

29   *from the wall of the hut. SHE holds it out.)* **Look. I've kept**

1   **it for you.** *(The bird trills again, and then again but SHE*
2   *can't find the source. SHE throws down the lute in*
3   *frustration. Angry:)* **Why do you torture me like this? You**
4   **went away, god damn you. You left me. You weren't here**
5   **to look after your son** *(SHE beats at her head.)* **Don't**
6   **remember, Marguerite.** *(SHE retrieves the fish and the*
7   *knife, and slices off another piece to eat. A wolf howls as SHE*
8   *starts.)* **The leaves are falling off the trees. I know what**
9   **comes next.** *(SHE panics.)* **I can't. Cold. Memories. Pain**
10   **far worse than the slice of a knife into soft flesh.** *(SHE*
11   *holds the knife over her wrist. Considers. The wolves cry*
12   *again.)* **No!!! I'll throw myself into the sea before I give**
13   **you fiends the satisfaction of picking my bones in the**
14   **snow!!** *(Tries to come back to reality:)* **No. No snow. Not**
15   **yet. No ice on …** *(SHE stops. Looks at the water.)*
16   **Something's on the water? Too dark for ice. It's a boat!**
17   **No. That's not right. You see things, Marguerite. You**
18   **know you do. Brightly coloured houses nestled against**
19   **the rocks. Large dinghies rowing out to sea and coming**
20   **back laden with fish. Visions. Nightmares.** *(SHE rubs her*
21   *eyes. Slowly looks again.)* **It's still there.** *(SHE gasps.)*
22   **They're dropping the sail. D'you think this time …** *(SHE*
23   *turns away. Looks back again.)* **They've come. They've**
24   **finally come for us. We're going home!** *(SHE waves and*
25   *signals towards the sea.)* **Herererere!** *(SHE runs around*
26   *gathering things up and throwing them down.)* **Damienne!**
27   **You can't be sleeping again! Get the baby ready. Get**
28   **Francis —** *(Looking for the child:)* **Francis?** *(Picks up a*
29   *rock.)* **I'll tell you a story. The great turtle made the earth**
30   **from his shell so Woman Who Fell from the Sky would**
31   **have a place to give birth to twin sons. One twin was**
32   **named Sapling or "He Who Holds Up the Sky." The**
33   **other was called Flint, or "The Crooked One." Sapling**
34   **gave the world berries and fruit. He also gave the small**
35   **animals which we can trap for meat to eat. Their bones**

1   and horns make tools and weapons and from their skin
2   and fur we can make clothes and bags. Sapling's twin
3   brother, Flint, gave the world the hunting animals like
4   the mountain lion and the bear. He gave the poison
5   berries and briars and plants that can make people sick.
6   But he also gave plants that can make them well. But I
7   didn't know how to — Oh, Francis! *(Drops the rock.)* The
8   ground was too cold to dig. And when the thaw came I
9   couldn't ... I couldn't ... *(SHE looks out at the sea.)* It's still
10   there. *(Pause.)* No. No! The boat Didn't come! Winter did.
11   You stopped making music, Eugene. You went out to
12   check the trap lines. *(Getting angry.)* My belly was huge
13   with child, and you didn't come back!
14
15
16
17
18
19
20
21
22
23
24
25
26
27
28
29
30
31
32
33
34
35

Sisters of Sisters
by Cynthia L. Cooper

1 Ginny — 13   Female — Serious
2
3 *(This play recounts the story of three pairs of sisters: two*
4 *women who really are sisters, and each of their two*
5 *daughters. They are all at turning points in their lives as they*
6 *struggle to define themselves and their sister-relationships. In*
7 *the following monolog, Ginny is standing outside the door of*
8 *her older sister's apartment. Ginny is trying to decide whether*
9 *or not to return home rather than spend the summer living*
10 *with her older sister, who is 20 years old. The monolog*
11 *invites a number of personal interpretations from the actor:*
12 *Does Ginny feel comfortable or uncomfortable now in her*
13 *older sister's company? Is her final exit an act of personal*
14 *independence, an expression of dislike towards her sister, or*
15 *a frightened avoidance of someone Ginny knows will want to*
16 *know "all about it" (the troubles in Ginny's life)? In any case,*
17 *the actress should avoid playing the piece as low energy,*
18 *dreamy recollections of childhood, because Ginny is really*
19 *wrestling with a very important issue at this point in her life.*
20 *What issue? The actor should invent a good one! And the*
21 *auditors should see Ginny as a young woman courageously*
22 *grappling with a problem and then standing up to make a*
23 *decision that is risky and uncertain, yet surely the best one*
24 *for her to make!)*
25
26 **I remember when I was only a kid — back in the sixth**
27 **grade. Mandy Pollack was my best friend, and we were**
28 **always writing notes to each other. And then one day I**
29 **went back to my desk and found a note, all folded up. I**

39

1   can still remember pulling each little fold out. And then
2   I read it. It said, "Dear Ginny: You've never really been
3   my friend. I hate you. Don't you ever talk to me again.
4   Mandy." Well, you gotta understand, I was just a kid
5   then, and ... well, I got sick. Literally. I had to leave
6   school and go home early. And when I got home, Mom
7   was there, and nobody else was, so I showed her the
8   note. And she just looked at it and kind of laughed. "It'll
9   blow over," she said. "It's just one of those grade school
10   things, don't you know." So I took the note back from
11   her and I went to my room and cried on it until all the
12   ink blurred. And then you came home, and you read the
13   note. Do you remember? And you know what you said?
14   You said I was a very good person and a much better
15   friend than Mandy and that I didn't deserve a note like
16   that. And then you started crying, too. Do you know
17   what I'm saying? You're the only person that's ever cried
18   for me, Cheryl. The only person. *(GINNY stands there a*
19   *minute, looks at the letter, then exits.)*
20
21
22
23
24
25
26
27
28
29
30
31
32
33
34
35

Boontown and
the Cinderella Cottonbrains
by Lynne Elson

1 Amelia — 18   Female — Comic

2

3 *(This extended monolog challenges the actor to believe*
4 *absolutely in the narrow but utterly charming point of view*
5 *of this young country girl. She is very talkative, even*
6 *rambling, and her narrative leads her through a wide range*
7 *of emotional responses. But what should amaze the listener*
8 *is that the whole story — including all the digressions —*
9 *hangs together and leads to an absolutely unpredictable*
10 *climax at the very end. Care should be taken to preserve*
11 *much of this "turnaround" at the end of the piece, if the*
12 *monolog is edited to a shorter length.)*

13

14 This here's just about the biggest celebration day of the
15 year. And it just happens to be my birthday. Did I eva
16 tell you this? The day I'z born my mama was cooking
17 supper. When she dropped her water, she dropped what
18 she was holdin', a carrot and two patatas. Landed in
19 such a way on the floor, lookin' like a man's body. Well,
20 just one part of it, if you know what I mean. My momma
21 saw it as a sign she agonna have a boy. She was so
22 excited. Everyone wants a boy, help with the work force,
23 help till a field. Heck, my brother Toby can shoe a horse
24 and build a fence — same time, don't have to learn to
25 be proper, or make sure he agonna get married off.
26 That's what I want, not ta have to worry about silly girly
27 things. But I'z not born yet. Let me get to that. I popped

41

1   out of my momma, playing stick ball right away, but that
2   didn't fool her. She and the doc knew I was a girl. So he
3   ask her what she was namin' me, and she said, "A
4   meal." She thought he said, "What were you makin'?"
5   I'm surprised I didn't come out called Hash or Goulash.
6   No, I got the name Ameal-ia. Tagged on some bows to
7   pretty things up. And I've been fightin' them things ever
8   since. Ya see, I didn't want nobody callin' me weak or
9   frilly, 'specially those stupid girls at school. I never
10   played house, and I didn't wear no dresses. That was my
11   rule, no matter how much I got a beatin' or how much
12   the girls all teased, I stood my ground wearin' Toby's old
13   pair o' pants tied round my waist with a rope to keep 'em
14   up. Now skip o'z about eighteen birthdays and you get
15   to today, Memorial Day — again. This time, though,
16   unlike all them frilly girls who are fussin' about what
17   they'z gonna wear, or which ribbons to put in their hair,
18   I'z doin' what I have to do. Prepare for the dancin'. See,
19   this birthday's special. Eighteen. Yep, that's me. And
20   see, this time, 'steada standin' outsidea the dance floor,
21   pretendin' I don't care, I'm gonna make somebody dance
22   with me. Even wash my hands first. If I haveta. I even
23   practiced. Yesterday, I was partners with a hoppity
24   bullfrog up by the crik. Couldn't get his slippery hand to
25   stay round my waist. But if I could make a hoppity dance
26   with me, I figured I cud make any boy. We was spinnin'
27   round and around. Then I heard it. Squeaking and
28   gigglin' and who could miss those petticoats scrapin'? I
29   tensed up. It was the cotton-brained girls. Knew they
30   were comin' to make fun o' me. They must have been,
31   'cause they never woulda made the trip down here with
32   all this dirty mud. This town had nothin' much to do,
33   'specially if you were a girl and wore dresses. All these
34   Cinderellas do all day is dream about boys. Wonderin'
35   which one's gonna ask 'em, who's gonna be theirs,

1 which one they can saddle an' tame. They'z all got yes
2 on their tongues but nobody been askin' yet. This year,
3 though, they all talk about how it's about time their
4 dreams come true. Makes me sick. Slowly they made a
5 circle 'round me. In front, the Cinderellas' leader was
6 Nellie-Morgan. I remember exactly what she says, she
7 says: "You'd be the worst wife on this planet, I bet even
8 drunk old Waste-a-way wouldn't marry you." That was
9 the lowest. Ol' Waste-a-way the town bum, roams
10 around and does nuthin' since his wife died. People said
11 he died that day too, probably why he smells so bad.
12 "What are you hidin' under those boy's clothin'," Marsha
13 bucktoothed Johnson spit out next. "Wh-wouldn't be
14 too sure you was a girl." Then they alls took up to
15 laughin', a grand ol' hee-haw and knee-slappin'. Stupid
16 girls, what did they know? They didn't know nuthin'. So
17 I'z gonna teach 'em. Right there, right in front of these
18 cotton-brained imbeciles, callin' me a boy and couldn't
19 even marry ol' Waste-a-way, and let 'em drop, zip, plop
20 'round my ankles. And I wasn't wearin' no bloomers
21 neither. So's you can guess how much their mouths
22 were flappin' then — none. Their lips were scoopin' up
23 pond mud, and their eyes were bulgin' right outa their
24 sockets. Big nose, freckle-faced Frances peed down her
25 leg. But I looked at Marsha and Nellie-Morgan and they
26 were just stone cold and I didn't think they really got
27 the full effect of the lesson. So I flopped my body down
28 to the ground and waved my legs in the air like a flag on
29 Flag's Day, so's they could get a better, more detailed,
30 look-see. Didn't know if those girls were gonna move
31 from that spot or sprout roots and grow flowers come
32 end of spring. Who cared? I hopped away, trailin' my
33 blue jeans behind me wavin' like a fancy tail. And today
34 I got up real early like. Couldn't wait to start the day. All
35 ready to see the parade, and bet on the hog races. Then

1 it hit me. I can't go. Nellie-Morgan musta spread through
2 town, all about me at the crick, quicker than Ma's blue
3 ribbon winning pie will get eat'n today. Darnit, I wanted
4 to go so bad. This was suppose-ta be my Memorial Day.
5 An' those cotton-brained petticoats gets to dance. I
6 hope they step on boys' feet. I'z so mad, I run outside
7 and kick rocks all the way down to the gate. When the
8 dust clears, I ain't sure, but, yeh, up the dirt road —
9 headin' this away, a huge crowd. It's all the boys of
10 school. I'z ready. I can take em. They'z getting' closer,
11 hmmmmm, what they holdin'? All them's got wildflowers
12 in their hands behind their backs. Hot damn! I'm a-
13 gonna get to go to the picnic after all! I can just see
14 Nellie Morgan's face when I walk into the picnic with all
15 the boys of town. And I'z not gonna let them dance with
16 nobody else all night long. They'z gonna all want to
17 dance with me — the girl who don't go no where 'cept in
18 pants.
19
20
21
22
23
24
25
26
27
28
29
30
31
32
33
34
35

Aurora's Motive
by Jamie Pachino

1 Hildegart — 18	Female — Serious

2

3   *(This character of Hildegart Rodriguez is based upon an*
4   *actual historical figure who lived in Europe in the early*
5   *1920s. An extraordinary young woman, Hildegart became a*
6   *noted lawyer, author and activist by the time she was 17*
7   *years old. In this speech she is shown during one of her*
8   *national lecture tours on the causes of sexual freedom, birth*
9   *control, socialism and the creation of the Spanish Republic.*
10   *This selection is very interesting because it can be played two*
11   *ways: either as a public speech with moments of great*
12   *passion and sincerity, as well as a final "personal appeal"*
13   *directly to the auditors; or as an extended monolog in a*
14   *conversation with two other characters. Either way, the actor*
15   *should not overlook the way the character struggles with her*
16   *self-doubt and overcomes her fears to press forward and find*
17   *answers for herself.)*

18

19   **Do we disdain progress? Yes, according to the current**
20   **social climate. By refusing to accept change. By**
21   **creating an extraordinary new entity, and then denying**
22   **it its own life. We cannot let go of the campaign, simply**
23   **because a single achievement has been won. Or why did**
24   **we fight so hard? If we relinquish the mantle once it's**
25   **been gained?** *(Trying again:)* **The greatness of Spain ...**
26   **Upon these issues ...** *(SHE looks out, receiving nothing.)*
27   **Are you listening? Do you hear?** *(SHE puts down her notes*
28   *deliberately, and moves toward the crowd.)* **Listen ...**
29   *(Intensely, trying to reach them:)* **When the Israelites**

1   escaped their captors of 400 years, they came to the
2   edge of the Red Sea. They turned to Moses, their leader,
3   and asked him why God had brought them so far, only
4   to let them perish at the hands of the Egyptians. And
5   you know what? Moses asked the same of his God. He
6   doubted. Until one man, one civilian, walked into the sea
7   past his waist, over his shoulders, all the way to his
8   mouth. And the waters opened and dry land appeared in
9   front of them, and the Israelites crossed to safety.
10   *(Deliberately:)* If you walk out of slavery, if you make a
11   journey so far, if you believe in liberty, you must be
12   willing to follow it, ferociously, blindly, and alone, until
13   you are covered in it. Only then will you know what you
14   are capable of. Only then can you find — freedom. *(SHE*
15   *looks out, searching, waiting. There is no response.)* I thank
16   you.
17
18
19
20
21
22
23
24
25
26
27
28
29
30
31
32
33
34
35

Duck Blind
by Shirley Barrie

1   Jenny — 14   Female — Comic

2

3   *(This amusing piece offers a fairly rich range of emotional*

4   *colors for the actor to express, all the while portraying the*

5   *"put-upon" attitude of a fourteen year-old who thinks her*

6   *family are geeks. Jenny is clinging to a floating duck blind*

7   *after being accidentally bumped off her family's boat in the*

8   *middle of a foggy night. There's no one around but a duck*

9   *who keeps quacking at her, and she keeps talking to*

10   *reassure herself — until the very end when her latent fear and*

11   *panic start to break through. The removal and donning of the*

12   *life jacket can be mimed, or a real life jacket can be used as*

13   *a helpful costume prop.)*

14

15   **Whoooo.** *(A duck quacks. JENNY jumps in fright.)* **Ahhh!**

16   *(SHE almost falls off the edge.)* **Geeeeeez! Now you almost**

17   **had me in the water.** *(DUCK quacks.)* **Don't worry. I don't**

18   **have a gun. Just a stupid crazy family. I mean I'm**

19   **hanging off the front end of the boat, right, trying to see**

20   **the channel through this blinking fog when wham — dad**

21   **drives into this duck blind and I'm gone. I thought I was**

22   **a goner. I had this split second, you know, when I was**

23   **actually grateful Mom made me wear this stupid life**

24   **jacket. But then I hear her screaming, "You've lost my**

25   **baby! Why aren't you backing up, you monster!" He**

26   **wasn't backing up because he thinks I'm in the water**

27   **and he doesn't want to catch me in the motor. But**

28   **that's a bit too complicated for her tiny brain. Not that**

29   **he's much better. "You all right, Kiddo?" he calls. Kiddo —**

1   like I'm still eight years old like stupid Lucy who just
2   blubbers. So I didn't answer. Well, I couldn't, actually. I
3   kind of got the wind knocked out of me when I landed.
4   Anyway, I just figure they can look for me for a while.
5   *(The duck quacks disapprovingly.)* **Well do you think I**
6   **wanted to come on this stupid moonlight cruise? If**
7   **they'd let me go over to Doug's house tonight they**
8   **wouldn't be riding around in the fog looking for me. But**
9   **oh no. "It's a school night, Jenny. You know we don't**
10   **allow that sort of thing." Like what do they think? That**
11   **we're having some kind of kinky sex and it's okay on the**
12   **weekend? I doubt it. They probably couldn't imagine**
13   **kinky. Anyway two hours later, Dad's bouncing around**
14   **the house, getting Lucy out of bed. "Great night for a**
15   **family moonlight cruise. Could be the last one of the**
16   **year. All hands on deck." Yeah sure. When it's**
17   **something he wants to do it doesn't matter what frigging**
18   **day of the week it is. I told him I didn't wanna come. I**
19   **hate it when they ask why in that tone of voice. Like it**
20   **doesn't matter what you say, presuming you even**
21   **wanted to say — they're not gonna buy it. I mean, I've**
22   **got my stupid period — for starters.** *(Duck quacks.)* **What**
23   **do you know about it? You lay eggs. They lock the**
24   **bathroom at night at the cheap-o marina. And this dumb**
25   **new boat of Dad's might have a cabin but there's still no**
26   **toilet. I'm gonna be a flooding mess by the time I get**
27   **home.** *(SHE feels her bottom, struggles out of the life jacket,*
28   *sits on it.)* **If I get home ...** *(Duck quacks.)* **Yeah, I know.**
29   **Fogs always lift. Eventually.** *(SHE shivers.)* **It's gonna be a**
30   **real barrel of laughs explaining to Katie and Sue that I'm**
31   **in the hospital with raging pneumonia because I spent**
32   **the night on a stupid duck blind 'cause my crazy father**
33   **has this retarded idea about family. "You used to enjoy**
34   **it," he says with that sort of sappy look in his eye. Yeah,**
35   **sure, that's what he thinks. I could die of exposure. And**

1   this rotten old blind could break loose and float through
2   the reeds. *(With increasing theatricality.)* **And** drift
3   towards the marina. Everybody's lined up along the
4   dock. But I'm beyond this world, floating towards them
5   like the Lady of Shalott. Okay so I'm not dressed like
6   her, but my face will be so beautiful and serene that
7   they'll see me with robes of white fluttering in the
8   breeze. Just like in that song Mom likes. She'll be
9   crying. Buckets. Lucy, the little brat, will be
10   remembering all the times she was so mean to me and
11   got me into trouble by playing all cute and innocent
12   when she's really a conniving little monster. Katie and
13   Sue are all teary — even Katie who's tough as nails.
14   And Doug is there, struggling not to break down. But he
15   lets out a heart-rending wail as my raft slides into the
16   dock. He leaps forward, throwing his arms around my
17   limp body. Mom and Dad are devastated. "Forgive me,
18   Kiddo," Dad cries. I'm dead and he's still calling me
19   some stupid baby name. But his face is all lined with
20   worry and grief. "We should have been more
21   understanding," Mom sobs. "If only we had another
22   chance." *(Duck quacks.)* Yeah. Only in my dreams. You
23   know, for one tiny infinitesimal second, I thought of
24   asking if Doug could come with us tonight. I must have
25   been mad. How could I even think of bringing somebody
26   I really like into contact with my crazy family. Doug'd
27   never speak to me again. For sure. Dad is just sort of
28   pathetic, but Mom ... ! She's afraid of everything. She's
29   specially afraid of the boat. She's forever pulling Lucy
30   and me back over the side and wringing her hands when
31   we water ski. She can't even swim! Well, if it's really hot
32   and we're anchored out at The Point — where the
33   sandbar is, you know — she'll get in the water and do
34   this truly embarrassing dog paddle. She doesn't always
35   come, but when she does she brings these amazing

1   lunches — stuff we love to eat whether it's good for us
2   or not. *(Catching herself:)* **And she moans a lot. When**
3   **Lucy was really small we used to gang up on her, Dad**
4   **and me. We'd do all this dumb stuff to scare the pants**
5   **off her. One time — I was about eight, I think — Dad let**
6   **me drive the boat right into the busy marina. She**
7   **freaked! And he'd let me ski when there were waves.**
8   **Anything more than glassy smooth and she's having a**
9   **hemorrhage! Even when she doesn't say anything, I can**
10   **tell. He understands what a thrill —** *(Duck quacks.)* **Okay,**
11   **okay. So maybe we used to have some good times. It's**
12   **just not the same any more. But they think it is. You are**
13   **so lucky. Weather starts to get down around freezing,**
14   **you just spread your wings and fly away down south.**
15   **Wish I could fly. Far away.** *(SHE waves her arms. Stops.)*
16   **Course, you do have to run the gauntlet of those asshole**
17   **hunters trying to shoot you out of the sky. Kind of like**
18   **parents, right? Aiming to shoot you down at every move.**
19   **Kapow! Any attempt to do something new. Kapow!**
20   **Kapow!! They should all be banned.** *(Pause.)* **Course, if**
21   **there were no hunters, there wouldn't be any duck**
22   **blinds, and I would have landed in the water which is**
23   **frigging cold and ... Having a rational mind can be a real**
24   **pain.** *(SHE recognizes her hunger.)* **I could use some hot**
25   **chocolate about now. Mom always brings real baby**
26   **marshmallows to sprinkle on top. Not those stupid dried**
27   **up ones that come in the packet. And she made her**
28   **"crazy dip". It is so good. She won't tell us what's in**
29   **it. "It's a secret," she says. "Maybe when you have**
30   **children ... "** *(SHE registers the silence.)* **Did you hear**
31   **something? A motor?** *(Pause.)* **No? Where are they? They**
32   **wouldn't go and ... Mom'd never let him leave me here.**
33   *(SHE calls.)* **Mom!** *(SHE frantically struggles back into the life*
34   *jacket. Louder:)* **Dad!!! It's me. Jenny!** *(Beat.)* **Your Kiddo!**
35   *(SHE looks out.)*

Mother, Tree, Cat
by Dori Appel

1   Beth — 20s   Female — Serious

2

3   *(Beth is an artist no longer connected to her art, a former child*

4   *prodigy who stopped painting in adolescence for reasons*

5   *known only to herself. In this speech she is older, telling her*

6   *favorite aunt about some of her most painful experiences as*

7   *an adolescent — experiences that help to explain the*

8   *alienation she now feels as a young woman. The monolog is*

9   *rich in detail and gives an actor plenty to visualize and*

10   *identify with. It challenges the actor to "set the stage" with*

11   *her story and narrate the poignant tale in an intimate yet*

12   *emotionally-charged, and bitterly humorous manner.)*

13

14   I assume we're talking about the same event, Aunt Liz:

15   the annual Horace Mann freak show, otherwise known

16   as Parents' Night. As usual, the star of the show is me:

17   Beth Irving, the adorable, smiling automaton. I'm now in

18   the sixth grade, but you'd never guess it to look at me.

19   My hair is still tied with ribbons in two little bunches,

20   and I'm wearing this old shirt of dad's to protect my

21   clothes — it hangs way down past my knees so I look

22   even smaller than I am, which in turn makes my talent

23   seem all the more amazing. Parents whose kids aren't

24   even in my class have all trooped in to watch me give

25   my famous painting demonstration before their very

26   eyes! Oh, don't tell me it was well-meant! It was only

27   meant to make my teacher and my mom and dad feel

28   important. So there we all are, Mom seated at one of the

29   desks, Dad hovering near the door to greet all the other

51

1 parents, you somewhere at the back of the room, so I'm
2 not even aware that you're there, and me painting away
3 at my easel, pretending not to notice this crowd of
4 grown-ups breathing down my neck. Eventually one of
5 them bursts out, "She's unbelievable!" Which is Dad's
6 cue to call from the doorway, "Keeps her busy." It's like
7 actors doing a choral reading in a play. "You must be so
8 proud!" they all chorus, and Mom and Dad chant back,
9 "It's a nice hobby for her." But I keep painting as though
10 this desperate little drama isn't happening, as though I
11 don't hear them exclaiming and burbling right behind
12 me. Finally someone says the magic words: "A genius!"
13 which send Mom and Dad straight to simultaneous
14 orgasmic heaven! Their daughter, their only darling,
15 beloved daughter is a bona fide genius! And then
16 suddenly I hear your voice. Talk about timing! "Genius"
17 is still hanging in the air, echoing like the last silvery
18 chords of a Chopin sonata, when your six words shatter
19 the moment: "Not too bad for a monkey!" And
20 everything gets very, very quiet. A monkey! A monkey!
21 And the scales fall from my eyes. For a minute I'm
22 absolutely stunned. I look at what I've been painting —
23 a still life my teacher set up for the occasion, and it's
24 completely flat. It's dead — a dead banana, a couple of
25 dead oranges, lying in a wooden bowl like corpses —
26 dead fruit in a round wooden coffin with a lifeless blue
27 cloth underneath. I look at my hand holding the brush,
28 and it's not like my hand, it's like the dried-up paw of
29 one of those little weird monkeys that organ grinders
30 have, the ones with miniature jackets and hats that
31 used to give me the absolute creeps when they took a
32 penny from my hand. I'm holding the paintbrush in these
33 paralyzed monkey fingers, and I can't move! And then a
34 strange sensation spills over me, which I don't have a
35 name for. This wild feeling of relief, because something

1   inside me is shouting, "You see! You see! None of this
2   has anything to do with me!" It only lasts a second,
3   though, because now another sound has entered the
4   shocked silence behind me: my mother is laughing — a
5   tiny metallic clink-clink-clink, like pennies falling into
6   the organ grinder's cup. Oh, she's quick! Her voice
7   piping up loud and clear to save the day: "Aunt Liz,
8   Beth's too big for that nickname!" Then Daddy vaults
9   over and gives me a big kiss. "That's my little monkey
10   face!" he says, and he and Mom laugh, and the
11   audience laughs — loudly, gratefully — and the fruit and
12   bowl and the cloth return to normal, and my hand
13   becomes my hand. I dab yellow paint on the banana like
14   a good monkey, and everyone sighs because I am a real
15   genius, and I haven't let them down.
16
17
18
19
20
21
22
23
24
25
26
27
28
29
30
31
32
33
34
35

Memory Gland
by Lynne Elson

1   Tam — twenties   Female — Comic

2

3   *(This short monolog captures very well the nervous, gossipy*

4   *mood of a neurotic character who needs to "get a life" and*

5   *stop obsessing about the little things. The actor shouldn't*

6   *parody Tam, or feel put-off by the trivial subject of her*

7   *narrative. Remind yourself that Tam actually believes*

8   *everything she's telling us, and the piece must be played*

9   *believably in order for it to work effectively.)*

10

11   Every time I'm in a bathroom, I think, don't sit, don't

12   dawdle, look around, be safe. My mother told me

13   something that made me scared to go to the bathroom

14   in public places. It wasn't my grandmother's constant,

15   "Did you wipe yourself?" until I was eighteen that did it.

16   It was my mother's story she told me. She said that she

17   went to the bathroom at a gas station once and she

18   squat, peed, and reached for paper. But she didn't see

19   paper. She saw a blinking eye on the other side of this

20   hole, cut out big enough so a Peeping Tom could see a

21   lady drop her drawers, and pop-a-squat. "So always look

22   before you pop-a-squat," was my mother's favorite line.

23   Luckily she had a tampon in her hand, which makes a

24   good eye-jabber. She says always use the plastic ones,

25   because they do more damage to the eyes than the

26   cardboard ones do. I guess they'd bend or something.

27   So let me tell you, it's hard enough peeing when I'm

28   worried about finding an eye behind a wall, but holding

29   a plastic tampon in one hand, squatting, balancing and

1 holding my pants up so it doesn't touch the floor — now
2 that's the stuff of circus performers. I'm telling you,
3 Ringling Brothers should hire me. And now I find out
4 that they have two-way mirrors in changing rooms! I'm
5 ordering everything over the Internet. Too bad I can't pee
6 that way, too.
7
8
9
10
11
12
13
14
15
16
17
18
19
20
21
22
23
24
25
26
27
28
29
30
31
32
33
34
35

Visiting
by Evan Guilford-Blake

1   Zhen — 19   Female — Serious

2

3   *(This monolog springs from Zhen's overpowering desire to*
4   *share with another listener her experience of visiting her*
5   *grandmother's grave. Although it begins ordinarily enough,*
6   *the first part of the piece must be infused with the same*
7   *enthusiasm that Zhen brings to the second part — the day is*
8   *too perfect, the clouds too white, the birds and butterflies too*
9   *carefree, and so on. As Zhen's excitement builds to the very*
10 *end, we begin to suspect that this is more than just a story that*
11 *happened in the past: it is a profoundly moving experience that*
12 *infuses the character's present life as well. The actor must*
13 *present the story with a great deal of "honesty" — overt*
14 *theatricality should be avoided. The piece moves from ordinary*
15 *storytelling through moments of curiosity and humor, surprise*
16 *and discovery, to the final moments, of confidence and joy.)*

17

18 **Last Sunday was my grandmother's birthday. I went out**
19 **to visit her — drove; the first time Dad'd let me take the**
20 **car to go anywhere outside the city — I just got my**
21 **license a few weeks ago; I had to wait 'cause I was —**
22 **sick the last couple of years.**

23   **It's not that far, maybe forty miles; just a little past**
24 **"civilization," just into the country. It's a pretty drive on**
25 **a nice day, and Sunday was beautiful. The trees'd just**
26 **budded, there were those little yellow flowers, I don't**
27 **know what they're called but they smelled wonderful, all**
28 **along the roadside. Just enough breeze so it was**
29 **comfortable to ride with the window open and listen to**

1 the whip of the wind 'nstead of the air conditioner. Not
2 a lot of traffic, which surprised me. But maybe that was
3 because I left early. The sky was very blue. Nimbus
4 clouds, lots of birds. Butterflies and birds.
5   I got there about ten o'clock, right when they
6 opened. I parked in the lot and walked; it's kind of a
7 long way — we're on the west side; it's the oldest part,
8 some of the stones go back to the 1800s. They had a
9 farm near there, my grandparents; a really successful
10 one. I laid the flowers I brought on her grave, and then
11 I just stood there a while. It was so quiet. Grandpa was
12 the one who bought all the plots — 96 of them! — so we
13 could be buried together, at least for a few generations.
14 And they're all marked — we all know where we're going
15 to spend eternity. Where our bodies will, anyway. Mine
16 is near the southern edge, right under a tree. I could see
17 it from Grandma's, the tree, and, and standing there?,
18 looking on it, I could imagine — no; no, not imagine: I
19 realized I knew what it was like, to lie there, in the
20 earth, to not know and, and yet to know: That there was
21 a world you'd been a part of, full of sadness and loss,
22 and laughter and love. I felt — I felt, for a minute, like I
23 did when I was in the hospital. I dreamed, in the coma.
24 I know I did, even if I can't remember them. But I
25 knew — something; when I woke up, I knew there was a
26 world — one where sight and sound and smell · didn't
27 matter — a world — apart, from this one, and I knew I'd
28 been a part of it, too. And even if I tried I would never
29 be able not to know that. It's funny — when I woke up,
30 the first thing I did?, was cry.
31   Anyway, I stood there, looking even though I think
32 my eyes were closed. Then I kissed Grandma — her
33 stone I mean — and I walked back. I didn't stop at my
34 plot, or at any of the other graves. I'll come out here
35 again; there's plenty of time.

57

Devils
by Linda Eisenstein

1 Agnes — twenties   Female — Serious

2

3   *(This challenging piece requires absolute belief by the actor in*

4   *the words that Agnes speaks to her friend, Mary Ann,*

5   *warning her about the evils of television. Although it sounds*

6   *like a sermon, the monolog gives the actor numerous*

7   *opportunities for physical actions to underscore the sense, and*

8   *ample opportunities to "invent" possible nonverbal reactions*

9   *from Mary Ann in order to energize Agnes's words in many*

10   *places. Remember that Agnes isn't crazy, she's just your*

11   *normal everyday neurotic person wondering what to do about*

12   *her television set. The actor should avoid playing the speech*

13   *like a harangue, and instead look for the many emotional*

14   *colors that Agnes displays in her attempt to persuade her dear*

15   *friend Mary Ann that there are devils in her TV set.)*

16

17   There's devils comin' out of there. I see 'em all the time.

18   Devils. They looks like they're human, but they ain't.

19   Not after they come outa there. You gotta be careful not

20   to look at 'em too close or they'll get you. Yes, they will.

21   We's livin' in dangerous times. Devils just tryin' to crawl

22   into every room of your house, every corner of your

23   mind. But I found a way. Praise heaven, I found a way!

24   To help keep them devils out of your house. Out of your

25   bedroom, or livin' room, or wherever you got that box.

26   Just don't turn it on, Mary Ann! Don't turn it on! I know!

27   I know you're used to it. I know everybody's got one. I

28   know you think them devils is your friends. Hell fire, girl,

29   don't you know that's their first step? To get you to

1   invite them into your house as your friend? Do you know
2   how much money they spend on that there box to make
3   you believe they's your friends? Thousands of dollars a
4   minute. Millions of dollars an hour. Millions. Of. Dollars.
5   To make you think them devils is your best friends. Well,
6   it ain't so. None of them wavy devils give's a rat's patoot
7   about you, darlin'. None of them wavy devils is goin' to
8   come over with a bowl of soup when you're sick, or hear
9   you if you fall down with a stroke, gaspin' for your last
10   breath, in front of that there box. They're just gonna
11   keep on movin' their wavy lips like you ain't there. They
12   ain't human! Not when they're comin' out of there. And
13   they ain't your friends! No matter how much they make
14   you laugh, or how many years you been watchin' them,
15   or how catchy their little tunes is. No matter how much
16   you think they keep the house from feelin' empty. The
17   house IS empty, girl! It's just full of you and some wavy
18   devilish voice. You're still by yourself. You just forget it
19   when they's comin' out of that box at you. All right. I
20   know they's not ALL devils. Every once in awhile they's
21   probably one that ain't a devil. I admit, you can learn
22   some good things on there. Some decent things. But
23   you gotta be on your guard. You gotta have ways to
24   figure out which ones it won't totally hurt you to look at
25   or listen to. First: you gotta watch 'em for awhile with
26   the sound off. That's one of the ways you can tell 'em
27   apart. Tell which ones might be human and good, and
28   which ones is human and just maybe a little confused,
29   and which ones is simply devils through and through.
30   Watch 'em without any sound at all. Then it's easier to
31   tell which ones is lyin' and which ones just want to suck
32   out your brain. I mean it! Turn off their yappin', and
33   you'll see it written all over their faces, plain as day.
34   Who wants to listen to devils like that? Like pourin'
35   poison in your ears. Like takin' a sitz bath in a septic

1   tank, that's what it is. All that hate and greed and
2   watch-me-fool-you-with-my-devilish-talk. It's a siren
3   song. So plug up your ears, darlin'. Watch 'em with the
4   sound OFF. Oh, yes, oh, yes. I do it all the time. That's
5   how I can tell which ones is devils. They's all over that
6   durn box. They give themselves all kinds of fancy titles.
7   Preachers. Senators. Mr. Expert this or that. Pundits.
8   Commentators. Talk show hosts, and talk show guests,
9   every kind of devilish talkin' head on the planet is in
10   there, yappin' away. Just watch their faces for a little
11   while, without hearin' the actual words. And pretty soon
12   you'll just about go crazy, realizin' how many devils is
13   out there tryin' to mess up your head and suck out your
14   brain. Suck it right out your eyeballs, into that there box.
15   Don't stare at 'em too long neither. It puts your brain
16   waves to sleep. That's right, it does! Right to sleep.
17   Rockabye. Might as well hit yourself over the head with
18   a two-by-four. Ever see a picture of the pattern your
19   brain waves make after fifteen minutes of that thing?
20   Flatliners. So help me. If that thing was a drug you
21   SWALLOWED instead of watched, there ain't nobody
22   could get it approved. No siree. So here's another trick.
23   You gotta pay attention to your eyes. Do special
24   exercises. Keep yourself from fallin' asleep and gettin'
25   flatlined. Like, for example: for five minutes, you only
26   watch out of one eye. Then you shake your head real
27   good. And in between those one-eyed looks, make your
28   eyes skitter all around the room — at the ceiling, at the
29   floor, at your kittycat or dog or anything but the durn
30   box. Set yourself an eggtimer. Now every five minutes or
31   so, when it goes off, switch your eyes again. Or turn your
32   head, so the box is behind you, and watch it backwards
33   in a mirror. Like you're lookin' at a vampire or a gorgon
34   or somethin'. Shake it up. Try somethin' different every
35   time. Jump up and down, call out bingo numbers, it

1 don't matter what. Anything to break up the pattern.
2 Just don't get flatlined! And don't fall asleep with it on!
3 You don't want them devils wormin' their way into your
4 dreams, do you? Flappin' their gums, givin' you one
5 hypnotic order after another, and you're rollin' your eyes
6 up in your head, goin' to sleep? Might as well lay down
7 in traffic. Put your head in a cement mixer. It'd be safer.
8 And, for the sake of all that's holy, keep your babies
9 away from it! Can you believe it, some folks stick their
10 children in a room hours at a time with them devils
11 spoutin' their evils? And you wonder why things is fallin'
12 apart at the seams? Hell fire, Freddie Kruger spends
13 more time with your little boy than his grandma does.
14 Rush Limbaugh rockin' your little baby to sleep. You're
15 out there all day, making four-fifty an hour, slingin'
16 hash, wonderin' how you're gonna get through the
17 month without standin' in line for government cheeze,
18 and goo-goo, he's watchin' some devil tellin' him he
19 needs two hundred dollar shoes and all girls is whoores.
20 And some other devil is sayin' you and all your
21 neighbors is lazy worthless scum and rich people need
22 more money. And there's pictures of slick silver
23 automobiles with leather seats that look like Satan's
24 pillows that cost more money than you can take home
25 in five years, and some devil is tellin' him he's supposed
26 to want one? Now what kind of idjit lets their children
27 look at such devilish mischief all day? You be better off
28 puttin' a brick through the screen and throwin' the durn
29 thing out onto the tree lawn and keepin' the plastic bag
30 it came in, let your kids stick their heads inside that
31 instead. It'd make as much sense. Let 'em play with a
32 rusty tin can and a dirty spoon, that'll hurt 'em less —
33 then listenin' to devils tell lies about the world all day
34 long. So many lies that you can't count 'em. So many
35 lies that you forget they're lies. Lies bought and paid for.

1   Made up and sold by a bunch of devils who are gettin'
2   paid more than everybody on your block put together!
3   While you sit there, you and your children, flatlined.
4   Shovelin' money at 'em. Suckin' your brain out your
5   eyeballs. While your neighbors starve. Devils! I can see
6   'em. I can SEE THEM. You know I'm right. You KNOW I
7   am. Look around. You KNOW what's wrong around here.
8   You KNOW. Yes, you do. You just think you can't do
9   nothin' about it. But it ain't true. You can do somethin'!
10   Get 'em out of your house. Out of your house! All them
11   devils. All them ... devils.
12
13
14
15
16
17
18
19
20
21
22
23
24
25
26
27
28
29
30
31
32
33
34
35

The Lesson
by Lisa Rosenthal

1   Girl — teens   Female — Serious
2
3   *(This girl struggles in the monolog to come to grips with*
4   *what she now regards as two painful learning experiences*
5   *years ago. She probably hasn't consciously engaged these*
6   *memories for some time, but it's necessary that she do so*
7   *now in order to remind herself of what she learned and apply*
8   *it to her present life. For dramatic effectiveness, the actor must*
9   *avoid playing the speech as a cold recollection of the past,*
10   *and instead remind herself that the memory and learning*
11   *experience is vividly part of the young woman's present*
12   *problems, which demand some resolution.)*
13
14   When I was a little girl, my grandfather grew very ill, so
15   ill in fact he couldn't see many people, or at least didn't
16   want to. It was probably ALS, although they didn't know
17   it at the time. So all the aunts and uncles got together,
18   and with my grandmother's blessing, decided I should
19   go visit him. I wasn't the only grandchild, but for
20   whatever reason they chose me. So I went, and I helped
21   Nanna. It was very difficult to see Papa the way he was,
22   all thin and frail, looking nothing like the grandfather
23   who read to me on his lap with his big burly arms
24   around me. I started making excuses to run to the store
25   or anywhere else that would get me away from him
26   because I was scared. He was scary. Eventually my visit
27   came to an end and Nanna writes me a letter telling me
28   how much she appreciated my help and how much Papa
29   looked forward to and enjoyed my visit. A week later he

1   died. I was nine years old. I thought I'd killed him, my

2   not wanting to be around him, my getting impatient with

3   his slowness, all of that made him feel unwanted,

4   unloved, like life had gone on without him so he wasn't

5   needed any more. Five years later my Nanna got sick. I

6   did't want to go. I knew if the aunts and uncles voted to

7   send me, well. They voted again; they sent me again. I

8   tried harder this time to be more patient with her than

9   Papa, more loving — I knew her life depended on it. But

10   I couldn't hold on to that. I loved her, but she wasn't the

11   same. When it came time to catch my plane I was so

12   relieved to be going home that I ran out of the car and

13   into the airport, forgetting to even kiss her goodbye. And

14   then she was gone. I'm older now. There are many things

15   I don't understand, but I learned that if I don't care

16   enough about someone, I can make them disappear.

17

18

19

20

21

22

23

24

25

26

27

28

29

30

31

32

33

34

35

Voices from the Shore
by Max Bush

1 Julie — 17   Female — Serious

2

3 *(Julie is an inpatient in an adolescent psychiatric ward,*
4 *speaking with Joel, also 17, who was just admitted to the*
5 *ward a few hours ago. Eager to re-establish contact with him,*
6 *she has fantasized about their relationship for some time, and*
7 *now her excitement pours out in the following speech. The*
8 *actor should avoid playing her "crazy," and instead should*
9 *look for more compelling motivations and emtions for Julie:*
10 *desperation, fantasy, lyrical joy, relief, affection, and so forth.)*

11

12 I couldn't help it. I didn't know what they wanted. They
13 were all yelling at me. I tried to listen to them all, I tried
14 to do what I was supposed to do. But ... this was me. It
15 was only me. And they could see it was only me. So they
16 hit me, again. So I asked to come here. To wait for you.
17 And now you're here. So I'm safe. And I can leave,
18 again, with you, when you tell me we are going. *(Singing*
19 *the word in delight:)* Goooooiiinnnnng. Goooooiiinnnnng.
20 *(Pause.)* I'm changing. Do you see? I'm older. I feel older,
21 too. I'm all new. It just happened to me. And I'm ready
22 for you, now. We won't go back where we were. We'll go
23 into our dream. When we were apart all those years, I
24 made a dream with you. And I told it to you, but I wasn't
25 sure you could hear me. If you didn't, I drew a picture of
26 it for you. Joel. *(SHE takes out a piece of paper, gives it to*
27 *him. Sings his name in delight.)* Joooooeeellll. *(SHE opens*
28 *the picture so he can see it.)* We'll live inside high, far away
29 walls. The walls will be so high no one can see over

1   them. No one will ever find us. The walls will look like the

2   sky, so no one will even see them. We'll live inside and

3   we'll have peacocks; I know you like peacocks because

4   you like their feathers: blue and green. We'll have a park;

5   our park; with a fountain and a pool, and I'll swim in our

6   pool and no one will hurt me this time. The fountain will

7   look like an angel. I'm ready, now. I wasn't before, but

8   now I am old enough and I can show you how to go there

9   with me. But you have to come, now. You have to come

10   soon, so I don't have to go with someone else. And now

11   that you are changing and you are with me, we are both

12   ready.

13

14

15

16

17

18

19

20

21

22

23

24

25

26

27

28

29

30

31

32

33

34

35

When Fat Chicks Rule the World
by Karen Mueller Bryson

1   Noreen — Indeterminate Age   Female — Seriocomic

2

3   *(This is a climactic monolog that gradually turns darker and*

4   *more cynical as it nears the end. The actor should avoid*

5   *playing Noreen unsympathetically however, as some kind of*

6   *"loser." Dramatic interest lies in the fact that she's honestly*

7   *struggling to understand and improve her situation. And her*

8   *positive qualities — a vibrant sense of humor, self-honesty,*

9   *energy, and imagination — need to remain foregrounded in*

10   *the presentation. In short, she's not an overweight woman*

11   *lamenting her situation; she's an attractive female who wants*

12   *to become thin and shapely.)*

13

14   Tuna. Sixty-six ounces. I wonder how many pounds that

15   is? Let's see. There are sixteen ounces in a pound, so

16   sixty-six ounces would be four pounds. I wonder if that

17   includes the can? Probably not. Wow — I'm the proud

18   owner of four pounds of fish. Surely, Margo and Jackie

19   don't really think I can eat all of this. Or maybe they do.

20   I know I'm fat. Every time I look in the mirror, that

21   person looking back at me reminds me of that fact.

22   Actually, I don't remember ever being thin. Mom said I

23   was close to ten pounds when I was born. Jeez — that's

24   two-and-a-half of these cans. I guess I was doomed from

25   the start. Girls like Margo and Jackie have it so easy.

26   They can get a guy whenever they want to and then they

27   discard him without thinking twice. I sincerely want a

28   relationship and I can't even remember the last time

29   that I even had a date. I know. It was Ernie Lumsden. I

1   answered his ad in the Lonely Hearts column. He said he
2   was interested in "substance" and "inner beauty". Yeah,
3   right. It hadn't even been five minutes that we were in
4   the restaurant when he excused himself to go to the
5   bathroom and never came back. That was really a lousy
6   thing to do. He was no Tom Cruise himself. Come to
7   think of it, maybe that doesn't really count as a date,
8   since we didn't really finish it — we barely even started
9   it. Maybe I can just have that date annulled. I wonder if
10 Margo or Jackie ever had a man walk out on them during
11 a date. Probably not. I bet they've done the walking. I
12 wonder if my life would be any different if I was thin? Who
13 am I kidding? Of course, it would be. I'd have a better
14 job. I'd probably be an executive in one of those big
15 offices downtown. I'd have a nicer apartment and a
16 better car. And a steady boyfriend. No — I'd probably be
17 married by now to a lawyer or a doctor. And I'd belong
18 to a country club where I'd play tennis every Thursday
19 afternoon. And people wouldn't make fun of me. No
20 more whispers whenever I walk into a room. No more
21 disapproving looks and snickering teenage boys. I
22 wouldn't be embarrassed to go to the grocery store. I
23 could buy ice cream without someone saying, "You don't
24 really need that." I could shop at any clothing store at
25 the mall. If only I looked like Margo or Jackie. If only I
26 was thin. I wish I was thin.
27
28
29
30
31
32
33
34
35

The Catechism of Patty Reed
by Bob Mayberry

1 Patty — 12-13   Female — Serious
2
3 *(Patty has survived the horrible winter the Donner Party spent*
4 *in the Sierra Nevada mountains by eating snow and the few*
5 *scraps of meat her mother left her. In this monolog she recalls*
6 *that experience years later, but the speech is more than a*
7 *distant recollection for her. Her struggle to give voice to the*
8 *terrible experience underlies every painful memory — at one*
9 *point she even turns to her doll and speaks through it as a*
10 *puppet. The actress must avoid losing herself in vague,*
11 *painful memories and sustain the desperate energy of the*
12 *piece by trying very hard to communicate Patty's feelings to*
13 *the world, in order to "exorcise" the character's "demons."*
14 *She holds a scrap of meat in her hand now as she speaks to*
15 *her only companion, her doll.)*
16
17 I eat snow. Every day it's something different. I pretend.
18 Snow biscuits. Snow milk. Snow potatoes. Snow soup.
19 Even ... even snow meat. *(In a rush:)* I didn't mean to eat
20 my dog, Billy, I didn't know, I mean I was hungry and
21 didn't notice what I was eating and I'll never ... *(Looking*
22 *at the meat in her hand:)* ... ever ... eat ... meat — *(Pause.*
23 *Then SHE shoves the piece of meat into her mouth and chews*
24 *it as fast as she can until she has swallowed it all. SHE licks*
25 *her hand, then her lips.)* I'm sorry, Billy. I'm sick of snow.
26 Mr. Breen told his wife not to feed me. There wasn't
27 enough for their children, he said. I watched them eat it
28 every night. Mrs. Breen took a spoonful of grey stuff out
29 of the pot — it smelled horrible — and fed the baby first.

1   Then a spoonful for each of the children. One for Jimmy.
2   One for Peter. And Simon and Patrick, Edward and ...
3   and the oldest boy, I don't know his name. *(Counting*
4   *them on her fingers:)* **Seven spoonfuls. I watched them**
5   **eat. Every night. I tried to curl up in the doorway, but the**
6   **wind came in under the flap. In the middle of the night,**
7   **when Mr. Breen was snoring, Mrs. Breen let me sleep in**
8   **the corner with the baby.** *(Holding her doll close:)* **It kept**
9   **me warm. She always saved a crumb of bread or piece**
10   **of hide I could suck on. She told me to never tell Mr.**
11   **Breen** *(SHE looks the doll in the face for a moment as if*
12   *making a decision.)* **We never told, did we? We've never**
13   **told anybody. And we'll never tell, will we?** *(SHE holds the*
14   *doll so it faces the audience and speaks in the doll's voice.)*
15   **It's our secret. Patty's and mine. We heard things, at**
16   **night. Sounds. Coming from the other side of the wall.**
17   *(PATTY suddenly puts her hands over the doll's mouth to stop*
18   *herself from telling. SHE speaks to the doll as her mother once*
19   *spoke to her.)* **Hush, baby. Everything is alright. Momma**
20   **and daddy promised. Momma and daddy always keep**
21   **their promises. Don't they?** *(Frightened by the thought:)*
22   **Everything was pretty. Pretty pretty white. I forgot about**
23   **being hungry while I sat on my rock and listened to the**
24   **ice cracking in the lake and watched the blackbirds fly**
25   **from tree to tree and watched for momma and daddy to**
26   **come down from the top of the white mountain and save**
27   **me. I imagined them like angels, dressed all in white,**
28   **floating down out of the blue sky and carrying me off into**
29   **the clouds where everything was pretty pretty white ...**
30   **pretty pretty ... white. I ate Billy. Mr. Breen ate the baby.**
31   **We lived. For awhile. Then there was nothing but snow to**
32   **eat. I died and angels came to take me to heaven. But**
33   **daddy fed me crumbs and ... and now I'm alive. I can't**
34   **hate them. He crossed the mountains. She saved the**
35   **meat for me. But how can I forgive them? I'll never forget**

1   what the world looked like when I was a child. Never
2   forget the taste of snow. Every night as I lay in bed I
3   hear Mr. Breen in the next room and I smell that smell.
4   I fall asleep remembering.
5
6
7
8
9
10
11
12
13
14
15
16
17
18
19
20
21
22
23
24
25
26
27
28
29
30
31
32
33
34
35

Love the Water
by Cathy Ryan and Katherine Burkman

1   Gloria — teens or twenties   Female — Seriocomic

2

3   *(This delightful piece offers ample opportunity for*

4   *physicalization, as Gloria encourages her boyfriend to join her*

5   *in a swim. It's a romantic piece that reaches its climax very*

6   *near the end. It challenges the actor in several ways: to*

7   *concretely imagine Robert's actions, to express her true*

8   *enjoyment of the physical activity of swimming, and most of*

9   *all to register the thrill as Robert gradually declares his love*

10   *for her.)*

11

12   **What do you mean it's wet? Of course, it's wet. Just**

13   **take one sock off, just put one toe in. You can do it.**

14   **There. Why are you shaking? It's eighty-two degrees out.**

15   *(SHE swims a bit in the shallow water.)* **For heaven's sake,**

16   **Robert, they throw babies in, newborns in, right from**

17   **the womb to the water — they swim.** *(SHE makes a loving*

18   *gesture to the water.)* **You see, you've got to love the**

19   **water. You can love it with a toe, a foot. You don't have**

20   **to do more than wade. Yah, I know this was my idea, but**

21   **we always do what you want.** *(Does a few water*

22   *maneuvers.)* **Yes, yes, I know it's cold, but you're in to your**

23   **waist and if you dunk you'll get used to it. It's like … like**

24   **falling in love. Just love the water, just a little. Yes, I**

25   **know the story about your friend — you've told me a**

26   **zillion times. Yes, yes, I remember, he got dumped out**

27   **of the boat and they couldn't find him and he drowned**

28   **and then they found him and brought him back to life,**

29   **only he lost all his hair and he was only twenty-one. But**

1 I'm here — you're not going to drown and you'll keep
2 your hair, I guarantee it! And anyhow, I think bald men
3 are sexy. No, no, if you do drown, I'll revive you with a
4 kiss. *(Spies a fish under the water.)* There's a fish — come
5 see, it's just under the water, not far. Come on. Don't
6 you think you'd better take your watch off. You can leave
7 it there on the rock. That's right, leave time behind. And
8 it's quiet. I mean really silent. We can finally be alone.
9 All you have to do is love it, just love the water. *(Offering*
10 *her hand:)* You want to hold my hand? No, no, I can see
11 you can handle it. You love the water, it loves you right
12 back. It holds you up — it holds you — no questions
13 asked. *(SHE goes under the water, then comes up to report.)*
14 There's nothing like opening your eyes underwater —
15 you see things so clearly. Try it. You see unexpected
16 things. The shimmer, maybe a turtle, well at least a
17 creature. *(Goes under and comes up spluttering water.)* You
18 can see me? You have your eyes open and you can see
19 me with my eyes open? I'm the creature? *(Goes under*
20 *again and comes up for air.)* Yes. You've just got to love
21 the water, Robert. And me!
22
23
24
25
26
27
28
29
30
31
32
33
34
35

Balancing
by Martha Lovely

1   Salina — teens   Female — Serious

2

3   *(In this moving conversation with her father, a high wire*
4   *aerialist, young Salina struggles to find the words to finally*
5   *break free of the parental forces that have been tearing at her*
6   *for so many years. The speech is complicated by the need to*
7   *play the locale as taking place atop a high wire platform,*
8   *where Salina is rejecting her father's encouragement to join*
9   *him on the wire, a few feet away. But her mother — her*
10 *Papa's former partner — has recently left them, and Salina*
11 *refuses to take her mother's place in the act. She loves her*
12 *father dearly, but she must express and declare her real*
13 *feelings — and identity — in the speech that follows.)*

14

15 I know it's simple, Papa. I mean, I know you think it's
16 simple, but for me it's not ... No, not because I'm so like
17 mother. Please! What do you mean? Of course, she was
18 insecure. Not up here. Down there. Up here was perfect
19 for her, for both of you. Wasn't it? I always thought that
20 was when you were happiest. I would sit down there, on
21 the bleachers below, watching you up here. "Come to
22 me, Frances," you'd always say. Then you'd gracefully
23 back away from her ... slowly, effortlessly. She would
24 move, even more slowly and almost as fluidly, as if
25 drawn by you, held to you by a thread. *(Slight pause.)* No,
26 I can't come to you, Papa — I can't take your hand now.
27 I'm really not afraid ... now. When you would both go up,
28 I was! Yes, I trusted you. Even when I was little, when
29 you were first training her. It was her I didn't trust. Oh,

1   Papa! I could tell! Up here she depended on you. You
2   were all she had, but all she needed, too. Sometimes I
3   didn't want to run up and dance along the wire with you,
4   no matter how much I missed you. Sometimes I felt like
5   you'd be better off without me, if you could just be you
6   two. I think that's what she felt, anyway. Yes, it is.
7   *(Slight pause.)* I know you love me, but me up on the wire
8   with you isn't going to change things. She's still gone!
9   Maybe that's one of the ways we're alike. Mama and me.
10   We both knew you'd be better off just as Dom and
11   Frances. She loved the attention. Those early days,
12   when she could join you up here, that was what she
13   really dreamed of, wasn't it? No, it wasn't about being a
14   family act. I knew, Papa, I could see it. Whenever the
15   two of you'd come down from practicing, and you'd call
16   to me, I could see the light go out of her eyes. It was like
17   she'd lost you. To me of all people. She couldn't see how
18   I wanted her to see me as much as you did. All she
19   could see was some of your attention belonged to me.
20   Don't make excuses for her! I will not take your hand!
21   *(Pause.)* I'm sorry, Papa. Can't you see? On solid ground,
22   we weren't enough. It's like instead of us multiplying her
23   love, we divided it. I don't want to do this. No, I will not.
24   No, I will not take your hand! ... Don't you see — I've
25   never been able to picture myself up here with you. This
26   has been her place, even since she left. I can't help it. I
27   don't want to leave you up here alone, but I don't want
28   to take her place either. How could I have told you?
29   What could I have said? Yes. I'm afraid of becoming like
30   her. I don't want to let you down. I can do it —
31   physically. I just ... it's not simple. It's different down
32   there, more complicated. But that's where I want to be.
33   *(Climbs down an imaginary rope ladder.)* That's where I
34   need to be!
35

Embalming
by Karin Diann Williams

1 Desiree — teens	Female — Serious

2

3   *(This piece is written to be spoken by a dead woman*
4   *describing the abuse that led to her suicide.)*

5

6   When I was three years-old, my Mommie left my Daddie
7   and we ran away to live at Gramma's in Chicago. When
8   I was four years-old, my Daddie followed us out to
9   Chicago and got a job with the telephone company, and
10   got us a four-bedroom house in the suburbs. When I was
11   five years-old, my Mommie left my Daddie and we ran
12   away to live at Auntie Ruth's in Miami. When I was six
13   years-old my Daddie followed us out to Miami and got a
14   job with the gas and electric company, and got us a
15   three-bedroom condo by the ocean. When I was seven
16   years-old, my Mommie left my Daddie and we ran away
17   to live in California, where we didn't know anybody, and
18   we even changed our names and everything. When I was
19   eight years-old my Daddie followed us out to California
20   and got a job at the cable-TV company, and got us a
21   two-bedroom apartment downtown. When I was nine
22   years-old, my Mommie went to the doctor and got a
23   bottle of little white tablets, and ate every one of them
24   up. Then my Daddie said it was too crowded with me
25   squeezed into the kids' room with my little brother and
26   sister. My Daddie said now that Mommie was gone,
27   there was plenty of room in the big bed with him. And
28   there I was. I have never, never forgotten my first night
29   sleeping in Daddie's big bed. I have never forgotten, for

1   a day or for an hour or for a second. ... there has never
2   been a day that I've woken up and I haven't remembered
3   and remembered and remembered. I am sitting in
4   school, and I feel the tender sore spot between my legs
5   where Daddie pressed his finger into me, and I feel the
6   blood seeping into my panties against the hard wooden
7   seat ... I am on the bus, and I look at my reflection in
8   the glass and I think of the bruises behind Mommie's
9   sunglasses, the dark places on her throat where his
10   fingers squeezed ... I am at a party and the smell of
11   Jack Daniels and seven-up in plastic glasses on
12   somebody's lawn makes me want to throw up, because
13   that was the way his breath smelled when he would
14   come to bed at night. I see a flower, and I remember the
15   roses, the delivery man climbing the steep, dark stairs
16   to the one-room walk-up where we're sitting in front of
17   the television, and me and my little brother and sister
18   are on a blanket on the floor with a pack of cards ...
19   There's a knock on the door, and she opens it, and
20   there's this delivery man with a dozen deep-red roses,
21   and she cries as she inhales them ... I remember it in
22   Chicago, I remember it in Miami, I remember it here.
23   Please come back, the note says. Please come back, I
24   love you. You know I'll always love you. I'll never forget.
25   In my grave I won't forget you. Every day, every hour,
26   every second is filled with you, for better or worse ...
27
28
29
30
31
32
33
34
35

The Maltese Frenchman
by Cary Pepper

1   Maggie — twenties   Female — Comic

2

3   *(This familiar situation of the starving actress plugging away*

4   *at a day job is all too familiar to young actors. Maggie's*

5   *monolog, however, challenges the actor to become an expert*

6   *storyteller and a comedian for much of the narrative, while*

7   *saving the real punch line — and its corresponding desperation —*

8   *until the very end. It also offers the actor an excellent*

9   *opportunity to devise her own vis-à-vis, and play off his/her*

10   *reactions as Maggie speaks. In the original play, Maggie has*

11   *just met a young man with whom she's been discussing*

12   *personal fantasies. He has just told her one of his, and she is*

13   *now responding.)*

14

15   I'm an actress. And you know what THAT'S like. MY

16   fantasy is to be in the right place at the right time, run

17   in to the right person, and get cast in something. Or at

18   least be asked to audition. Because let me tell you, I'm

19   GOOD. But of course that never happens.

20

21   You know what it all comes down to? Control. How much

22   other people have, how much you have, but most of the

23   time, how LITTLE you have! It's always about who's

24   calling the shots. It's all jumping through hoops! Or

25   trying to CONTROL the hoops. Even a job like this. It's

26   not your typical, soul-eating, nine-to-fiver, but ... "You

27   Name It, We Do It"?? What is that? A polite way to say,

28   "I'm a servant"? A nice way to say, "Here I am, abuse

29   me!" Because you should see some of the things we are

1   asked to do! Some of the stories I could tell you ... All
2   right, I WILL tell you a story. I'm called to this
3   apartment, and there are these two guys, the one who
4   lives there, and his plumber. Who turns out to be his
5   brother-in-law. And for the first five minutes, all they do
6   is say to each other:
7   "It leaks."
8   "It don't leak."
9   "It does leak."
10   "It don't leak."
11   "It leaks."
12   "It don't."
13
14   Then the conversation begins to get a little more
15   interesting.
16   "It oozes."
17   "It oozes?"
18   "Yeah. It leaks so slow you can't see it."
19   "Then how do you know it's leaking?"
20   "I know. I seen it."
21   "You just said you can't see it."
22   "Yeah. But I seen it."
23   "How do you know it leaks, if you can't see it?"
24   "Believe me, it leaks."
25   "How do you know?"
26   "I seen it."
27   Okay, they exhaust all THOSE permutations. And it
28   turns out "It leaks" wants me to watch the faucet, to
29   prove to "It don't leak," that it does leak. "You think you
30   can do that?" What I think is, this is a joke! But no —
31   he's serious! "It don't leak" won't take his word for it,
32   so he's brought in "a disinterested third party." Then,
33   "It don't leak" turns to me and asks, "You know us?"
34   "I've never met either one of you."
35   "So you don't know us."

1   "Yes, that, too."
2   So, THEY go to a baseball game, and leave ME to watch
3   the faucet. *(Pause.)* Now, you could say what's the big
4   deal? There are a lot harder jobs I could have gotten.
5   Like the time I had to take a 300-pound, highly agitated
6   St. Bernard to a cat show! Or you could say, I HAVE
7   BETTER THINGS TO DO WITH MY TIME!
8
9   But a pay check is a pay check. So I sit there, staring at
10   the faucet. And nothing happens. I sit, and I stare and I
11   stare and I stare ... Nothing.
12
13   And then I see it ... The tiniest drop, peeking out at me.
14   And slowly it gets bigger and bigger, becoming more
15   visible. And it begins to take shape ... filling out, getting
16   rounder, fuller, fatter. Like a caterpillar emerging from a
17   cocoon. And finally, it's a big, fat, swollen pearl, so big
18   and round and heavy I don't know how it's staying up
19   there ... And then it doesn't ... it drops off, and I can
20   actually see it falling, as if my perception has been
21   heightened. And it falls ... down ... down ... down ... and
22   then ... splat! It hits the sink. And I start to let out this
23   huge whoop of joy, because I have done it! I got the
24   proof! I did it! And ...
25
26   I realize I'm getting excited over a drop of water! And
27   something is REALLY WRONG with this picture. Because
28   look at the utter, complete CRAP I am doing ... ! And it
29   isn't even MY crap! It's THEIR crap. It's important to
30   THEM! Like the woman who sent me out to get a box of
31   rainbow paper clips that was available at only ONE
32   store, and who made me sign a CONFIDENTIALITY
33   PLEDGE before she would tell me where the store was!
34   What do I care where they sell rainbow paper clips!? To
35   me it's just an errand! It's a JOB! It's a DAY JOB! Not

1 a CAREER! I HAVE a career! And it ISN'T going to the
2 store, or doing your laundry, or buying your wife an
3 anniversary present, or meeting your cousin at the
4 airport ... or watching your faucet drip!!!
5
6 I am an ACTRESS!! I am a GOOD actress!!! And ...
7 *(Now completely calm:)* ... this has NOTHING to do with
8 what we were talking about.
9
10 BUT THAT FELT REALLY GOOD!
11
12
13
14
15
16
17
18
19
20
21
22
23
24
25
26
27
28
29
30
31
32
33
34
35

MONOLOGS FOR MEN

80 Teeth, 4 Feet and 500 Pounds
by Gustavo Ott

1   Angel — 20s   Hispanic Male — Serious

2

3   *(Angel is a young ball player who has been up against it in*

4   *the U.S. for nearly a decade, and can't seem to make it on*

5   *any of the major teams. Now in his mid-twenties, he has a*

6   *wife and child, and doesn't know what to do. He tries here*

7   *to explain to his friend, Fossa, an older Hispanic player who*

8   *is now relegated to scouting for the majors, how the team*

9   *managers have been giving him the runaround. Fossa has the*

10   *unpleasant task of explaining to Angel that as long as he's*

11   *not a U.S. citizen, he'll have to give up his dream of playing*

12   *major league baseball.)*

13

14   No, you don't know the situation, Fossa. I got two

15   apples I steal back at the hotel and a cold acid that

16   drills into my bones. Fossa, I'm running out of money.

17   There's no job openings. I got two apples and this green

18   frog coat that make me look like a Salvadorian batboy

19   about to be deported, a zombie in an old movie, a

20   delinquent, a green immigrant shadow that's just the

21   right size for a dumpster, living like a drunk, can't speak

22   no language at all, 'cause I can't even talk Spanish no

23   more. A green scarecrow ready to be deported to

24   Saturn, stuffed with lucky charms, I'm a green imported

25   man, a infiltrator that lives off Social Security, pulling

26   scams on the system to see if I can get away with some

27   crumbs. I'm green Spanish-speaking bad breath

28   clogging up the lungs of this green city. I got two apples

29   I steal in the hotel and a cold acid that drills into my

1   bones. *(Pause.)* I looked for work. In a pizza place. I carry

2   sacks of flour. I know the owner with her yellow teeth

3   and fat legs, her job is to humiliate the employees. And

4   the nice Italian man who does her a favor and sleeps

5   with her in exchange for two days off. "Mister, would you

6   be so kind and carry up ten sacks of flour in three

7   minutes?" TEN SACKS OF FLOUR, mi amigo. You think

8   I got any life left for baseball after TEN SACKS OF

9   ENRICHED FLOUR? *(Pause.)* I just want to play ball.

10   *(Pause.)* No, you don't know the situation, Fossa. I got

11   two apples I steal back at the hotel and a cold acid that

12   drills into my bones.

13

14

15

16

17

18

19

20

21

22

23

24

25

26

27

28

29

30

31

32

33

34

35

Pee-Pipe
by Sandra Dempsey

1	Jimmy — 18 Male — Comic

2

3   *(This amusing selection runs about three to four minutes, but it*
4   *can easily be edited down for a one- to two-minute presentation*
5   *by concentrating only on the last third or the last half of the*
6   *speech. The year is 1942, and the scene is the Royal Canadian*
7   *Air Force Training School. Jimmy is a trainee, seated in the*
8   *forward cockpit of a two-seater training aircraft. The actor*
9   *should note the way in which the monolog subtly changes*
10   *from an intimate conversation with the audience to a*
11   *"flashback" as Jimmy vividly re-lives the embarrassing incident*
12   *with his mother. The monolog is filled with minor "triumphs,"*
13   *moments of humor, items of curiosity, and rhythmic variety*
14   *before building to a hilarious conclusion at the very end.)*

15

16   If ya wanna know what flyin' is all about, here's the
17   gumph. Flyin' is all about stuff that ain't supposed to,
18   fallin' from the sky. Doesn't matter what th' job is, if
19   there's an aeroplane up there, ya know there's gonna be
20   stuff comin' down here. I mean, sure, there's the obvious
21   stuff like guys parachuting an bombs gettin' dropped.
22   But I'm talkin' all the other stuff nobody ever mentions.
23   Like throwin' out any an' everythin' that ain't nailed
24   down t' help lessen yer weight an' gain altitude — like
25   dumpin' fuel t' lessen yer chance o' fire; bombs, too,
26   getting' dumped where they weren't meant to be
27   dumped. An' guns — whew-wee! It's not just th' actual
28   bullets that rain down eventually, but the shell-casings,
29   too! Thousands of 'em! Oh, an' o' course, there's always

1   guys pukin' — I mean, why puke into yer lap when ya kin
2   just lean over ... ? They just never show that kinda stuff
3   in th' picture-house news-reels — all's they show is
4   good-lookin' flyboys all manners an' snappy salutes. But
5   ya never see all th' poor saps duckin' fer cover on th'
6   ground! Ya just never know what's gonna come down on
7   yer head in this war. But I'll tell ya the biggest secret in
8   the whole flyin' world. One o' th' first things ya get
9   introduced to in the cockpit — any plane — Tiger Moths,
10   Harvards — doesn't matter. They all got ... well, it's a ...
11   a kind of ... Well, it's a pee-pipe is what it is. Y'know,
12   so's a guy can let go if he has t'. I mean, it's not like ya
13   can just pull over to th' side of a cloud ... It empties
14   right out the' bottom o' th' fuselage — usually out of a
15   fancy-lookin' pipe. You'd think it was some kind of
16   sophisticated mechanism, stickin' outa th' aircraft like
17   that ... well, I guess it is vital! 'Problem is, the flyin'
18   hours are so short, even th' long-haul trainin' — y'know,
19   cross-country 'n all that — well, none of us ever gets a
20   chance to figure out how t' use th' pee-pipe before we go
21   off solo. Now, in my case, *(HE nods towards the aft*
22   *cockpit.)* me an' my instructor are just wrappin' up
23   maybe our third-t'-last dual-instruction together ... Dual-
24   instruction — yeah, that's where th' ham-fisted student
25   pilot, me, tries to figure out how t' fly this brand new
26   bird, harness th' six hundred horses behind th' prop and
27   make her soar sweet, like a hawk — while the flight
28   instructor, *(HE indicates behind.)* him, pretty much
29   guzzles Milk o' Magnesia an' holds on fer dear life. *(HE*
30   *begins to land the aircraft.)* So I bring me an' my instructor
31   down in that Harvard just as pretty as th' press in his
32   pants. An' just as I bring us into th' flight line, he throws
33   back the perspex, an' starts climbin' out, before I've
34   even got her to a stop, an' yells, *(HE imitates the instructor,*
35   *yelling above the engine noise.)* **"Yer doin' alright, kid! Go**

1 on! Re-trim an' swing her round an' take her right back
2 up fer a circuit! She's all yours!" An' he gives me a good
3 hard slap on my back an' jumps down off the wing. My
4 solo check-out! Holy jumpin'! First in my class! All th'
5 guys are crowdin' around t' watch! My heart's thumpin'
6 so hard, I could spit! An' by now, the ground crew an'
7 everybody are startin' to get mighty interested in how
8 come I'm sittin' there like a dope in a flight-hot kite an'
9 not getting' her chalked an' re-fueled. *(HE does the*
10 *following.)* So I re-trim ... an' I gun her good an' loud just
11 t' make sure I got everybody's attention ... I taxi out ...
12 an' they clear me an' give me th' green right off ... I give
13 her full throttle ... an' ... I unstick ... An' I'm soarin' like
14 a friggin' bird! Solo! *(HE does the following.)* **Gear up** ...
15 retract flap ... I'm so excited! ... ho-hoooo! ... *(His*
16 *bladder suddenly fills.)* ... **Oohh jeeze! I gotta go!** I had t'
17 take a leak when we landed, but I didn't wanna say
18 anything an' get him browned off ... **Oh jeeze! I gotta go**
19 **so bad my back teeth are floatin'!** What'll I do? I can't
20 hold it! I'm gonna wet my pants! Wait! Th' pee-pipe!
21 Where's th' pee-pipe!? There! *(As HE ducks down and*
22 *fumbles for the pipe, the plane dips.)* **Whoah, jeeze, keep**
23 **her nose up, man!** *(HE recovers control with his right hand*
24 *on the stick.)* **Straight an' level** — everybody's still lookin'
25 — keep her straight an' level! Oh, but jeeze! You idiot!
26 He said do a circuit, not fly to China! Jeeze! Th' kite's
27 fuel tanks are near empty an' mine are gonna burst!
28 Wait! I know! I'll put her into a nice, three-sixty orbit 'til
29 I figure things out down here — they'll think I'm just
30 show-boatin'. *(HE inclines into the left-hand turn.)* **Oh**
31 **jeeze! I'm gonna burst!** *(HE fumbles to unzip his fly.)*
32 C'mon, c'mon, c'mon! Jeeze, th' zipper ... I've never
33 been so left-handed! Oh jeeze! C'mon! Jeeze, I don't
34 remember it bein' so small ... ! I am not climbin' outa
35 this bird with a wet monkey-suit! *(As he connects the*

1   *pipe:)* **Oh thank you! Thank you, lord! Oh, thank you!**

2   **Oh ...** *(While HE continues his jettison operation, HE glances*

3   *casually out at the ground below.)* **Huh! 'Looks like a**

4   **farmhouse. 'Looks kinda familiar — Hey, wadd'ya know —**

5   **Dad's got an old red Chevy just like that one! An' a**

6   **vegetable patch beside th' house — we've got the same**

7   **thing at our place! An' there's a lady — huh, looks like**

8   **she's hangin' out washin' on th' line — I guess**

9   **everybody's mom does th' laundry on Monday! ... now**

10   **she's, she's lookin' up here — look at that! She's wavin'**

11   **to me!** *(HE smiles and nods his head at her.)* **Yes, I see you!**

12   **Hello to you, too, Missus! I'd wave back, only I kind o'**

13   **got my hands full at th' moment. Uh-oh — Maybe she's**

14   **not wavin' to me after all. Looks more like she's shakin'**

15   **her fists? She is! She's mad as a hornet!** *(HE laughs.)*

16   **What's th' matter, lady? My aeroplane too noisy for ya?**

17   **Did I wake ya from yer beauty sleep? Well you just take**

18   **a good look at my registration number under th' wing an'**

19   **see if they pay any attention to ya when ya complain!**

20   **There's a war on an' this happens t' be official airforce**

21   **trainin'! Hoo-hoo! Get a load o' those chickens runnin' all**

22   **over th' place! Hey, lady! Am I scarin' away yer dinner?**

23   **Hey, wait a minute — we've got chickens at our place!**

24   *(Recognizing the woman:)* **Oh my gosh! Mom!? MOM!?** *(HE*

25   *simultaneously loosens his grip on the pipe and the control*

26   *stick.)* **Whoa, jeeze!! Don't let go now, ya jerk!! Oh,**

27   **jeeze! I knew our farm was close to the airbase, I just**

28   **never realized how close ... Oh, please don't remember**

29   **the registration numbers, Mom! Please don't! Oh my**

30   **gosh — how many other guys have been doin' th' same**

31   **thing?! If th' war isn't over soon, our own civilians are**

32   **gonna drown! Oh, jeeze! I'm piddlin' on my own mother!!**

33   **I gotta stop ... Oh, like I can stop ...** *(Pause.)* **Here I am**

34   **gettin' ready to serve my country, an' all this time, I**

35   **thought it was th' hard water makin' our sheets yellow ... !**

Dear Mother and All
by Sandra Perlman

| 1 | Murray — 21 | Male — Seriocomic |

2

3 *(This monolog is based on an actual letter sent home from a*
4 *young American flier during World War One, a pilot in the*
5 *famous "Lafayette Escadrille." The text reflects a certain*
6 *naiveté about air combat, partly that of the writer and partly*
7 *that of the historical period in which he lived. But this is part*
8 *of the monolog's charm. The actor should project just as*
9 *much excitement by the events narrated here as Tom Cruise*
10 *does in the famous film "Top Gun." Though not at all a*
11 *situation like those encountered by jet fighter pilots today,*
12 *the same surprise, the same pride, the same mystery and*
13 *confusion and relief at the end of a long flight are part of*
14 *Murray Spidle's wartime experiences, just as much as they*
15 *are a part of our world today.)*

16

17 **We fly four or five hours, twice a day. One trip's usually**
18 **to escort a bombing squadron and the next time we go**
19 **way over the Hun lines, mostly looking for trouble. When**
20 **we set out across Hunland, they bang away with Archie:**
21 **dat-dat-dat-dat-dat-dat-dat! That's anti-aircraft guns,**
22 **and as long as we're getting arched we don't mind so**
23 **much. I know that sounds funny, but it's the quiet, when**
24 **everything suddenly stops, that can drive you crazy.**
25 **Then a fellow spends an agonizing two seconds, which**
26 **seems like an eternity in these gas kites, trying to see**
27 **where those Huns are and when they're going to hop on**
28 **you. I got into my formation the other night and was**
29 **traveling along our lines watching an artillery duel when**

1	all of a sudden I saw this hail of bullets coming at me. It
2	was then I discovered I had accidentally crossed into "No
3	Man's Land." I tell you, that's one place you don't ever
4	want to be. I sure did scamper back fast. But you never
5	want to get caught over there too long because there's
6	no room for accidents in "No Man's Land."
7	
8	
9	
10	
11	
12	
13	
14	
15	
16	
17	
18	
19	
20	
21	
22	
23	
24	
25	
26	
27	
28	
29	
30	
31	
32	
33	
34	
35	

Written in Water
by Bob Mayberry

1	Man — late teens Native American Male — Serious

1   Man — late teens   Native American Male — Serious

2

3   *(This is a stepping-stone monolog that does not contain great*

4   *dramatic "peaks" or dark "valleys" of the soul. Instead, the*

5   *actor must play the speech honestly, questioning everything*

6   *that he describes. In fact, the most vivid emotion is perhaps*

7   *contained in the boy's description of his grandfather's*

8   *reactions to what the boy tells him at night after work on the*

9   *pool deck at a Vegas resort in the 1950s. The boy seems both*

10 *fascinated and repelled by the whites who waste their*

11 *resources in the desert, just as he seems fascinated by — and*

12 *impatient with — his grandfather's disbelief of the boy's*

13 *descriptions of how the whites live in their fancy hotels. But*

14 *he cannot ignore the whites, any more than he can ignore the*

15 *warnings of his grandfather.)*

16

17 **Grandfather says there was a river here once, but**

18 **Grandfather says a lot of crazy things. He says when the**

19 **whites first came here, our people thought they were the**

20 **lost brothers told of in the old stories and dreams. The**

21 **ancestors rushed out to greet the wagons, arms wide**

22 **open like birds ...** *(HE demonstrates.)* **... but the whites**

23 **shot them. Grandfather says we didn't know what guns**

24 **were then. I can't believe it. Arms wide open? Why? To**

25 **hug them? I would sneak up at night and steal their**

26 **pockets. Whites have all the money in the world in their**

27 **pockets. I find it every day. See that man bringing the**

28 **woman in the two-piece swimsuit a drink from the bar?**

29 **Money's in the back pocket of his swim trunks. When he**

1   sits down on the lounge chair, the heavy coins will fall
2   out. I'll be picking up towels near there in a minute. It's
3   easy. White people are careless. They waste everything.
4   But you don't go running at them with your arms wide
5   open! Grandfather has a story — no one believes it —
6   about the river he says was here once. Here, in this
7   desert? He says the whites drank it. That's why all the
8   water is gone. I tell him he's wrong. I tell him how the
9   whites sit around and stare at the water with drinks in
10   their hands. Don't lie, he says. Whites are too busy
11   making their bombs to sit around and stare at water, he
12   says. I tell him to come and see. Come with me to my
13   job, I say. Come to the deck where I gather towels and
14   see the water. Little crazy one, he calls me. Each night
15   after work I fill a tin can with water from the pool and
16   carry it home, to the colony where we live, just across
17   Main Street near the park. I carry the water to show
18   Grandfather, and because we have no water except what
19   we carry. The well went dry last year, when they first
20   filled this pool with water. I'd like to jump in, feel the
21   cool water all over me, drink so much I'd never be thirsty
22   again. But they won't let me. No Indians in the pool, they
23   say. So I pick up towels and save the coins they drop
24   and watch the pink clouds from the bombs they make
25   float across the sky. It's kinda pretty. But Grandfather
26   still doesn't believe me about the water.
27
28
29
30
31
32
33
34
35

The Visible Horse
by Mary Lathrop

1 Scott — 12   Male — Seriocomic
2
3   *(This has been the worst year of Scott's life. Not only did his*
4   *father die in a car accident, but his mother moved them to a*
5   *new city, away from everyone and everything familiar. This*
6   *should give the actor something concrete upon which to*
7   *build an imaginary character biography. Scott's mother has*
8   *also been in need of support: she seems to merely be going*
9   *through the motions of parenting and can't really see how*
10   *her behavior is forcing Scott to parent her. In the original*
11   *script, Scott delivered his monologs on a bicycle, on in-line*
12   *skates and on a skateboard so the audience could see him*
13   *metaphorically "working to maintain his balance.")*
14
15   **Watch this ... See? ... No, wait, watch this ... See, cool,**
16   **huh? This is cool ... Anyways, I figured out what being**
17   **cool is. It's ten percent popularity, ten percent fashion —**
18   **and that includes such as hygiene. Right? Also your**
19   **hair, how you smell and bad breath. Hey! no! Nobody**
20   **wants to talk to somebody with green teeth. See? White,**
21   **right? And you should do three baths a week, only I'm**
22   **on swim team, and chlorine kills underarm germs, so I**
23   **don't take baths, cuz of the chlorine — hoo, I'm really**
24   **glad of that. But I wash my hair in the shower after**
25   **practice, right?** *(HE takes a small sample size bottle of*
26   *mouthwash out of his pocket.)* **This is my mouthwash —**
27   **Scope.** *(HE swills some in his mouth and spits it back into*
28   *the bottle.)* **Did you know you can use it more than once?**
29   **Just swoosh and spit it back — a course, you gotta spit**

1   thin or you'll spill. Anyways, I've had this Scope since
2   school started. It showed up in the mailbox, and my
3   mom, she goes, "Hey, go ahead and have it." And it's
4   still minty fresh. Still! Want to smell? *(HE puts the bottle*
5   *back in his pocket.)* So, ten per cent popularity, ten per
6   cent fashion, and that includes what your wear, your
7   shoes, oh!, *(HE squats down and ties his shoelaces.)* **High**
8   **tops are cool, but don't lace them all the way: Uncool.**
9   Anyways, the laces, you know, the laces are too short to
10   tie that way. I think if the tongue's all messed up, see?
11   That's pretty cool. *(HE takes a comb out of his pocket and*
12   *combs his hair.)* I got a haircut. Haircuts are pretty cool.
13   Only, see, I was gonna let my hair grow. I seen this
14   picture of my dad when he was little, our age, and his
15   hair waaaay long — man, it was awesome. I think he was
16   a hippie or something. So I go, "Yo, Mom, I'm gonna
17   grow my hair long, like that." And she goes, "Forget it.
18   Nobody wears long hair anymore." Only when she takes
19   me, we walk in, and the barber, right?, he has this hella
20   long ponytail half ways down his back. For real! And I go,
21   "So, Mom! Nobody's got long hair!" She was psyched
22   out! And this hippie barber, he goes, "All the cool guys
23   have short hair." So I go, "Yeah? Guess you're not cool"
24   Right? And my mom, I thought she'd shit. I'm not
25   kidding. And this barber goes, "I may not be cool, but I
26   know what is cool. And short hair is cool." No, he was
27   way cool; he wouldn't take shit. So I go, "Okay." Right?
28   Only when he cut it, this hippie barber, he cut my
29   sideburns which I did not want. Anyways, I comb it back
30   with gel, which smells good, and that's hygiene. Gel's
31   way cool. Do you want to smell my haircut? *(HE puts his*
32   *comb back in his pocket.)* So, ten per cent popularity, ten
33   per cent fashion, and eighty per cent attitude. My mom
34   goes, like, "Yo, be friendly." Puhhh! You got to know who
35   to take shit from, and who you can waste right back on.

1   You gotta know. With most kids do this: neutral, see? Or
2   you can smile just a little, see? Most kids like if you
3   look neutral or friendly. But with some kids, do this.
4   Heck, you gotta! If you do this on one side, it's snarling,
5   and that impresses them. A course, you do it on both
6   sides, you could start a fight, right? Anthony, this mean
7   kid, every time, well not in front of teachers, in front of
8   teachers he's sooo polite — I hate this guy. I was taking
9   a pee in the boys' bathroom, and he was taking a pee
10 beside me, and he goes, "Ooooo, now that Jason taught
11 you karate, why don't you beat me up?" But all those
12 boys in Mrs. Winslow's homeroom ... there's Josh and
13 Chris, who everybody thinks is great, and Anthony's
14 maybe tight with them. I don't know, but they're a tight-
15 knit class and they don't take shit. They're all really
16 tight, and if I wasted Anthony, they'd all waste me. I
17 could waste him. I could. If my dad was here, I know
18 how he'd go. Like he'd go "Yo, Anthony, you pick the
19 time, you pick the place, I'm gonna beat the crap out of
20 you, you little shit." My dad, he'd, he'd go like that. Oh!
21 And, like, if your friend is the smallest kid, and
22 someone's wasting him, and you're big, right? You gotta
23 stomp on that bully, cuz its your friend. People see you
24 stick up for some guy and that's popular. Also,
25 sometimes they'd waste on you so you have to waste
26 back. They do that to prove you, and then they'll let you
27 in. That can happen. It can. That's it: ten per cent
28 popularity, ten per cent fashion, eighty per cent knowing
29 who you can waste. The best kids to waste are new
30 kids, cuz they don't have any friends, but I think that's
31 mean. Heck, I wouldn't waste some guy just for being
32 new. His mom probably made him move, and he didn't
33 want to, right? Like, he really wanted to stay at his old
34 house, with his old friends and his old school, but his
35 Dad got killed, and his Mom wanted a fresh start. Naw,

1   you shouldn't waste some new kid, cuz you might find
2   out that his dad got wasted and his mom made him
3   come here even though he didn't want. And now he has
4   to live in a condo, and they gave away his dog. I would
5   probably be nice to a new kid — except if he dumped shit
6   on me, I'd punch his guts just once so's he'd know I'm
7   tough. Then we could be friends. And, maybe, he still
8   has his bike, and we could ride bikes, do hobbies. That
9   would be cool. Know what? At my old school, building
10 models was a hobby. A lot of guys built models, and me
11 and some of my friends, sometimes we'd build together,
12 even. Like this one time, me and my dad invited over my
13 model friends and we built the visible horse. It was
14 awesome. He looked just like a horse, only his skin was
15 clear plastic and you could see all his plastic guts. And
16 my dad, he goes, "Let's eat horsemeat burgers for
17 lunch," which grossed us way out. And after, we brought
18 it in and showed and telled. See, model building was
19 known. I don't think anybody builds models at this
20 school, so shhhhh. Right? So, ten per cent popularity,
21 ten per cent fashion and hygiene, right? And eighty per
22 cent attitude. Like if somebody stomps on you, you gotta
23 stomp back or you're a wus and that's not popular. Oh!
24 And staring. Staring's the worst. If someone stares at
25 you, don't look away. If you look away, hoo, you're in for
26 shit forever. I do staring in the mirror, to practice, right?
27 You gotta practice, cuz you gotta look evil. They get way
28 psyched if you look evil. Man, I hate staring — it's really
29 hard. Oh! and, check this: even girls do staring ... but I
30 don't know why. They stare weird, right? And you can't
31 waste girls or you'll get shit forever, right? Anyways, I
32 don't think you should ever waste a girl. I mean, I don't
33 like them, right? but I probably will next year. They had
34 this dance in the gym, right? No parents allowed — it
35 was awesome! You had to pay three bucks to get in, but

1   then you could eat all the chips and crap you wanted. I
2   only danced once, by myself. When they dance fast,
3   everybody just dances, and that's pretty cool. Hey, I
4   wouldn't dance slow for a million bucks! Oh! And this
5   girl stared me. I'm not shitting! I stared her back way
6   evil, but she stared me for a half an hour. Every time I
7   looked, she stared me. I was psyched. My mom, she
8   took me, right? but I wouldn't let her walk me in, cuz no
9   parents allowed. Anyways, she made me wear this black
10   shirt; she said it was cool. She shouldn't say that, right?
11   When she says "cool", it's lame. But I wore my
12   Simpsons shirt underneath, so I took it off. Simpsons
13   shirts are fashion, but you gotta wear a clean one every
14   two days — that's hygiene. They had the lights turned
15   way down at the dance and a strobe, but it was waaaay
16   noisy. That mean kid, Anthony, he wasn't there — see,
17   he really is a wus. *(HE nods his head, as if in time to
18   music.)* Head banging: I did this for the whole dance.
19   That was being cool. Every time that girl stared me, I did
20   this. *(HE demonstrates a staring face.)* They only played
21   two slow dances, right at the end, cuz they couldn't find
22   the slow dance music. Mr. Edwards, he was in charge of
23   the music. Mr. Edwards, he's okay. If we get him for
24   science next year, that would be really cool. You know
25   what he does? Dissects cow eyes. Gross! That would be
26   awesome. I could of slow danced that staring girl, but
27   they only played two, right at the end. What if my mom
28   seen? See what I mean, right? If my dad was here, I
29   would have danced her. My dad was cool. My mom! My
30   mom would go, like, "Who's that little girl you danced?"
31   But like, "Yo, Mom, stay in the car." So, ten per cent
32   fashion and hygiene, ten per cent popularity, eighty per
33   cent attitude. But, hey!, with girls, I think it's ten per
34   cent popularity, ten per cent fashion, and ten per cent
35   hygiene. See what I mean, right? With girls you get an

1   extra ten per cent for hygiene. And you can't be gross to
2   a girl, cuz they get really grossed. Like you can't talk
3   about cow eyeballs and such — they don't think it's cool.
4   Girls don't like being grossed, right? If I slow danced that
5   staring girl, I'd go like, "Do you like my Simpsons shirt?
6   It's clean." Right? Girls like stuff like that. And if her
7   breath was bad, I'd let her use my Scope. That's
8   friendly, and that's popular. Oh! You want to see
9   something? *(HE takes a rock out of his pocket.)* It's got gold
10   in it. See? Little tiny flecks of gold, for real! Hey, I found
11   it at my old house. Me and my dad, we were digging this
12   hole, and I just found it, right? See? And my dad, he
13   goes, "Awesome! Maybe it's a magic rock. If you make
14   one special wish, it might come true." I go, "Dad, chill —
15   I'm not a baby. Magic rock? It's gold, and that's good
16   enough for me." Right? I'm gonna keep it 'til I'm twenty-
17   five, then I'm gonna sell it. Make fifty thousand bucks
18   from one rock. I'm gonna give it to my mom. Like, "Yo,
19   Mom, here's fifty thousand bucks. Buy a mink coat."
20   Right? *(HE puts the rock back in his pocket.)* I found that
21   with my dad; it could be magic. You ever had magic? Not
22   that wussy, fakey stuff, like cutting a lady in half. My dad
23   said that was fakey. I mean real magic, like some things
24   in nature have power, right? I was wishing on this star at
25   my old house, stars have power — until I found out it was
26   a street light. Duhhh. You can't wish on streetlights.
27   Well, you can, but you don't get nothing back — I found
28   that out. I could wish on this rock, right?, like, if it really
29   did have power. You know were-things? Like werewolves
30   and werebears and vampires? They're way cool. The
31   undead: creatures that are living and dead at the same
32   time, I believe in that. I do. You can be living and dead.
33   You could be both at the same time, right? And if you
34   could wish a guy back from beyond, that would be
35   awesome, right? So's, I'd wish for my dad. My mom, she

1 goes, like, "Always remember your dad." "Yo, I'm not
2 stupid, Mom." She goes, "You're gonna be all right.
3 You're gonna grow up and be a fine man like your dad.
4 That's what he'd want." Hey, my dad didn't care if you
5 were fine or nothing. He liked you anyways. He'd go,
6 "Yo, nobody's perfect. Give me five." He'd go like that.
7 Unless you messed with his stuff, then he'd go, "Hey,
8 man, that's my stuff: put it back." He'd go, "Anthony's
9 an asshole." He'd go, "You're my best pal." He'd go,
10 "It's okay if you dance that staring girl. You can dance
11 her if you want." So, you want to chill? Wanna see my
12 condo? *(HE exits on bicycle.)*
13
14
15
16
17
18
19
20
21
22
23
24
25
26
27
28
29
30
31
32
33
34
35

The Visible Horse
by Mary Lathrop

1   Scott — 12   Male — Seriocomic

2

3   *(This shorter monolog by the same character as in the*

4   *previous, longer selection, focuses upon Scott's pained*

5   *memory of his father who was killed in a car accident. The*

6   *same background information mentioned above with the*

7   *previous selection applies to this monolog as well.)*

8

9   Can I tell you something? It's kinda scary. 'Member I

10 told you I'd wish my dad back from being dead, right?

11 Anyways, last night I snuck a star candle, shaped like a

12 star, matches and such. This was way late, okay? I got

13 out my magic rock I showed you, this picture of me and

14 my dad camping, and my dad's T-shirt I stole from the

15 dirty clothes a long time ago. See, sometimes I miss my

16 dad at night, is all. Only when I lit it, the match goes

17 pooooosh, man, this helluva huge flame from this little,

18 tiny match, right? And my lamp goes out. I go, "Shit!"

19 The candle, it goes pooooosh! It was waaay bright. And

20 check this: I didn't light it with the match, and it

21 wouldn't blow out. So heck, if magic comes, you're

22 stuck with magic, right? I go, "Yo, spirits, I want my dad

23 back." Right? I go, "Yo, spirits" three times. Three's

24 magic. Nothing. So I go, "Yo, Jesus, I want my dad

25 back." I go, "Yo, Jesus" three times. Then I go, "Magic

26 rock, full of gold, make my dad appear." See, my dad,

27 my dad, he knew, he knew it was magic, right? And the

28 candle, right? The candle goes out. It was dark, heck,

29 not even my night light — I don't even know what

1   happened, but it was waaaaaay dark and scary. And
2   then I hear something, whoa, it was bad. Cchhhhh ...
3   Cchhhhh ... Cchhhhh" I was freaked! "Cchhhh ...
4   Cchhhh ... " I mean, what is that? "Cchhhh," right? And
5   I go, "Who's calling, please?" I go, "Oh, shit!"
6   "Cccchhhhh." Anyways, I keep a flashlight under my
7   bed. Only when I stick my head under, I feel hair. I'm not
8   shitting. Thwonk! There's green glowing from under my
9   bed, and it's my dad, yes! Holding my flashlight. I go,
10   "Dad! What are you doing here?" And my dad, he goes,
11   "Cccchhhh." And he spits out this helluva hair ball. It
12   was, like, this big. Then he reaches up for me, right?
13   And he goes, "Help me out."
14
15
16
17
18
19
20
21
22
23
24
25
26
27
28
29
30
31
32
33
34
35

Listen to Our Voices
by Claire Braz-Valentine

1   Luis — 16   Male — Comic

2

3   *(This monolog is really in two parts: the first section up to the*

4   *point where the babysitting story begins, is spoken by the*

5   *entire cast in the original play; then the second section is*

6   *spoken by Luis. It can be shortened by editing-down in this*

7   *way, if time is a requirement. On the other hand, the two*

8   *sections can be performed as a unit, as the monolog appears*

9   *here — in which case the actor gains the opportunity for*

10   *strong contrast. The rhythmic first section can be done almost*

11   *as a rap, followed by a very naturalistic commentary —*

12   *directly to the auditors — about babysitting one's brother. It*

13   *is a high-energy piece, and Luis undoubtedly knows how*

14   *funny he really is.)*

15

16   Parents tell you when to eat, what to wear on your feet,

17   when to sleep. Don't drink beer, don't pierce your ear.

18   Do your chore. It's such a bore. Clean the kitchen. Stop

19   your bitchin'. Clean your room. Use the broom. The

20   garage is a mess. I hate your dress. Clean the house. I

21   hate your blouse. Wash the clothes. Your friends I

22   loathe. You forgot to walk the dog. You always eat like a

23   hog. Wash the car. Don't go far. Water the plants. Hike

24   up your pants. Grocery shop. Use the mop. Don't smoke

25   grass. Show a little class. Your music stinks. Don't take

26   any drinks. Don't get sexual. Be an intellectual. Fix your

27   awful hair. Don't let me hear you swear. Time to wake

28   up. You need a little shake up. Come home on time.

29   Don't commit any crime. Don't get high. Don't ask why.

1   Do the dishes. Grant my wishes. Don't give me
2   resistance. I'm responsible for your existence. You
3   better change your ways. You're going through a phase.
4   You will be my ruination. All this of my creation. Don't
5   make up another story. Don't say again that you're
6   sorry. Just shape up. Just wake up. Just clean up. Just
7   be good. For god's sake be good. You really should just
8   be good. I've got to say that most of time I think I try
9   with my family. I mean I even do chores. Well some of
10 the time I do chores. The worse possible chore is baby-
11 sitting. Now I really like my little brother, JoJo. He's
12 just learning how to talk and man some of the things he
13 says you know, they really crack you up. But when I'm
14 watching him, like when I'm supposed to be taking care
15 of him? I just don't understand it because the minute
16 we're alone, he takes one look at me and then guess
17 what he does? He loads his diaper. Now that's really
18 sick. And he just walks around pretending that it didn't
19 happen. Now I know he knows, I mean how can you not
20 know? Just thinking about it makes me want to throw
21 up right now. He does it on purpose. He looks me right
22 in the eyes and then he loads his pants. Then he just
23 goes right to his toys and wants me to play with him.
24 That's so sick. And the smell! Damn, now that's
25 something. He's so little. How can he smell so bad?
26 Every where he walks it's like this brown cloud is over
27 him and pretty soon the whole house is stinking. But he
28 doesn't care. He just strolls around *(HE strolls around*
29 *looking cool, walking like a teenager, not like a baby)* **as if**
30 **nothing happened. Sometimes he walks with his legs a**
31 **little far apart like this.** *(HE does this, but not as a baby*
32 *walk, as a cool teen walk, but with legs apart.)* **Maybe if I**
33 **just wait till my mom comes home I can say I didn't**
34 **smell anything. Maybe I'll open all the windows and**
35 **doors and then the smell might blow out. Then you'll**

1   never guess what he does. I can't stand it. Just as if he
2   doesn't have this big old load in his pants he sits down.
3   Then I can't believe my eyes cause then like this stuff
4   squirts out the side of his diaper! Then what am I
5   supposed to do? Talk about nasty! One time my friends
6   came over when I was watching him and gets this cool
7   idea. He shakes his leg like this. *(Shakes one leg.)* Well of
8   course, JoJo does the same thing except this little piece
9   of poop falls out of his pants. Rolls right and across the
10   kitchen floor. I thought we'd die we laughed so hard.
11   Course my brother thinks now he's got this real comedy
12   act cause he's walking around the house shaking his
13   legs and this stuff is falling out all over the place. We
14   were laughing so hard I thought we were going to throw
15   up. Then my mother walked in. She didn't laugh. That's
16   the thanks you get.

17
18
19
20
21
22
23
24
25
26
27
28
29
30
31
32
33
34
35

War of the Buttons
by Jonathan Dorf

1 Siggy — early teens   Male — Serious

2

3 *(In this monolog, Siggy is speaking about his escape from*
4 *Bosnia to three of his new friends in the American town where*
5 *he now lives. This challenges the actor because the images are*
6 *so powerful, and in order for it to work it cannot be played as*
7 *a vague dream or as a casual memory. Nor can it work if*
8 *played in a sort of emotionally dulled monotone, as though*
9 *Siggy were still denying the past. Siggy makes a great effort*
10 *to recall these buried memories, and he suffers great pain in*
11 *expressing them to his friends. But only by struggling to bring*
12 *them out in the open and grappling with his emotions, can he*
13 *hope to lay the painful memories to rest.)*

14

15 When the war happened, they came through the village,
16 and if the people already killed had anything worth
17 money, the soldiers would take it. They'd strip the
18 bodies. The men and boys that were alive they'd bring
19 together, and in some villages shoot them. That's what
20 we heard from people running from the army, people
21 who came through our village. Naked dead bodies,
22 clothes in a pile. *(Pause.)* When we found out the soldiers
23 were coming, my father told me take off all my clothes
24 and put them in a pile. He and some of the other men
25 did the same, and my mother and the other women told
26 the soldiers that their army had already been through.
27 *(Pause.)* We thought if they saw the bodies with no
28 clothes, they'd think we were dead and they wouldn't
29 bother with us. I had my eyes open, like I died with my

1   eyes open, because it was the only way I could see if they
2   were looking at me. To breathe. I tried to hold my breath,
3   and when I had to breathe, only do it when I was sure
4   nobody was looking. *(Pause.)* My father — something, a
5   butterfly — landed under his nose. He sneezed. A soldier
6   thought he wasn't quite dead and put a bullet in his
7   head. A butterfly killed my father. And my mother tried
8   not to, but she got so ... so much crying, that they shot
9   her. I laid — lied — lied there naked until the soldiers
10   left. *(Pause.)* In a month, they snuck me out. *(SIGGY finds*
11   *some salt in his pants pocket and throws it over his shoulder.)*
12   Being naked ... it's like being quiet ... it makes you
13   invisible ... it makes you safe.
14
15
16
17
18
19
20
21
22
23
24
25
26
27
28
29
30
31
32
33
34
35

Passion
by Chris Woods

1	Carlos — 14+	Hispanic Male — Comic

2

3   *(This monolog contains a great deal of storytelling, as well as*
4   *strong moments of surprise and discovery as the actor*
5   *reaches the end of the piece. There are also serious moments,*
6   *as well as self-revelatory parts here and there that offset the*
7   *comedy of the piece. It's a ladder-type of monolog, so the*
8   *actor should also be very attentive to pacing it properly and*
9   *building to a climax while rehearsing it.)*

10

11   Ola! I'm Carlos. I just got famous. Oh, I know what
12   you're thinking. That Carlos Cortina could never amount
13   to much. Sure, I've heard it all. My dad? He's over in
14   Paradise Graveyard on account of getting a knife
15   between his ribs. And my brother, Manuel? He's in
16   prison for borrowing cars without asking. Manuel's
17   kinda famous himself. Maybe you know about him? Me,
18   I'm gonna make something of my life. That's what I told
19   mama, and she believes me. Who else is gonna take
20   care of her? You know, she just got that new aluminum
21   leg, on account of her arthritis? Yeah, that makes two of
22   those metal legs she's got now: mama says she's ready
23   to go dancing. All she needs is a new boyfriend. I'm
24   helping her build her confidence. Yeah, things have been
25   going good for me. I'm staying out of trouble, and I think
26   I've got a new girlfriend. Yolanda Perez. You know her?
27   She's pretty special. We've been at Sisters of Mercy for
28   three years. But it wasn't until today that she looked at
29   me twice. See, I heard Father Cantu was looking for a

1   suitable Jesus for the Good Friday Passion ceremony.
2   Oh, I didn't give it much thought at first. But mama said
3   I should try out. For her, she said. Hey, I like doing
4   things for mama. She's had a rough time the last few
5   years. In fact, I quit sniffing that Liquid Paper stuff on
6   account of her. And you know what? I feel better. So I
7   guess playing Jesus was like another step. I don't mind
8   telling you, Father Cantu was plenty surprised to see
9   Carlos Cortina show up. He knows about my dad and
10   Manuel, so he wasn't expecting too much from me. But
11   he said he'd give me a chance. He already had some guy
12   to play Barabbas. I figured that was like Manuel in the
13   olden days. Oh, mama was so proud! Her and Tia Clara
14   came to watch. They were like celebrities! I had to wear
15   this crown of thorns. It looks a lot worse than it feels.
16   They gave me this white robe with chicken blood
17   spattered all over it. The blood was to show how Jesus
18   got whipped by those Roman dudes. And they made me
19   wear this diaper thing. Pampers, I guess. After I put this
20   on, I remembered I wasn't wearing my jockstrap. Like
21   Father Cantu told me? Oh well, it was too late to do
22   anything about it. Things got started. I had to drag that
23   big old cross around the churchyard, then across the
24   football field. They told me to go slow 'cause the
25   crucifixion wasn't supposed to happen till noon. So I
26   bent over like an old man and dragged the hell out of
27   that cross. People were everywhere, following me.
28   Women were crying their eyes out. These guys dressed
29   up like Roman dudes were pushing me around the whole
30   time. At noon they laid me down on that cross. They
31   stretched out my arms and tied me down with ropes.
32   They stood the cross up. All hell broke loose then. The
33   sky turned black, just like the real thing. There was
34   thunder and lightning! People were crying like crazy,
35   especially mama. 'Bout then I looked down from my

1   cross, and there she was. Yolanda Perez! She was
2   looking up at me with that beautiful smile. And she
3   said, "Hi, Carlos." Well, that just about made me come
4   down from that cross. Maybe take her to a movie. Or
5   something. At first I couldn't figure out why she was
6   smiling. Then old Father Cantu came hurrying up with a
7   pole. He poked it right under my diaper and started
8   rearranging things. *(HE wiggles around.)* That's when I
9   figured out why Yolanda was smiling. *(Beaming:)* It was
10   like advertising! And the prettiest girl at Sisters of
11   Mercy was smiling at me for the first time! I was in
12   heaven! I was hanging on that cross for an hour. After
13   awhile I forgot all about the people crying and carrying
14   on. All of a sudden it was like I could see for a long, long
15   ways. Over their heads. Over the town. I saw dad's
16   grave over at Paradise. I saw Manuel sitting in his prison
17   cell. I could see for miles and miles. I guess what
18   happened was, I could see my future. And you know
19   what? I liked what I saw! And I decided some things. I'm
20   gonna take care of mama. I'm not going to steal cars.
21   And I'm not gonna get a knife between my ribs. I'll even
22   finish school. And Yolanda Perez? Ay! We got a date for
23   Sunday. You know what she said when I asked her out?
24   She said, "Don't forget your diaper, Carlos." And then
25   she winked at me! I guess this is all part of being
26   famous. Hey — it doesn't get any better than this.
27
28
29
30
31
32
33
34
35

The Masked Tenor
by David LeMaster and Derald Mabbit

1   Joey — 20s   Male — Comic

2

3   *(This monolog develops from a mood of amusing recollection*

4   *to enthusiastic storytelling at the end. There is also a certain*

5   *amount of puzzlement, genuine incomprehension in the*

6   *speaker at his fate as a comedian when seen against the*

7   *career of the other vaudevillian. Joey also finds his stories*

8   *amusing — particularly the tale of the Siamese twin act. But*

9   *as the "confession" of an actor-comedian, the piece is*

10   *excellently suited to establishing an intimate rapport with the*

11   *audience during the enactment. The actor shouldn't hesitate*

12   *to share the range of emotions — resentment, astonishment,*

13   *amusement — with the spectator at every opportunity.)*

14

15   **Duck McShays was five-feet-one-inch, had fire engine**

16   **red hair, buckteeth, and a lisp. He played Shakespeare**

17   **on vaudeville. He'd come onstage with this skull, see,**

18   **and sashay around and then lisp like a little fairy, "To**

19   **be, or not to be! That is the question! Whether 'tis**

20   **nobler to bear the whips — ow! And scorns — oh! Of**

21   **time." People used to hoot and holler and throw things**

22   **at him. One night somebody threw a tomato and hit him**

23   **square in the face. Duck let the juice drip right off the**

24   **side. The next night he came to the theatre wearing a**

25   **suit made out of linoleum. They sold vegetables at the**

26   **door. For an encore he cleaned himself. One night**

27   **Duck's partner was sick, so the director asked me to go**

28   **on with him in the famous Siamese twins act. There**

29   **were three legs to the suit, see, so we each put a leg**

1   down the middle. Once we got into the suit I turned to
2   him and said, "Look, you touch me and I'll pelt you one.
3   Got it?" So he waited until the curtain was rising and
4   then he goosed me. So I popped him on the nose. The
5   lights went on and the audience saw one half of a
6   Siamese twin beating the crud out of the other half. And
7   Duck, blood dripping from his nose, jumped out of the
8   suit and screamed, "Whip me, scorn me! Whip me,
9   scorn me!" He got three curtain calls that night. The
10 S.O.B. He could make people laugh reading out of the
11 phone book. I hated him. And then one night the
12 director came in and said Duck McShays had killed
13 himself. Said he left a note about some guy who
14 wouldn't take him seriously. How he hated it when
15 people laughed at him. Here I was, sweating every night
16 to be funny, and this S.O.B. kills himself because he
17 can't turn the funny off. I was jealous as hell!
18
19
20
21
22
23
24
25
26
27
28
29
30
31
32
33
34
35

Pressure
by Lindsay Price

1   Alex — 17   Male — Serious

2

3   *(Alex is a refugee from Belarus. He's trying to explain to his*

4   *friend Ally why he can't go to the school dance. The actor*

5   *should play a strong vis-à-vis here: a young girl who has no*

6   *conception what it's like for Alex, coming from a country in*

7   *turmoil and trying to adjust to the normal everyday life of a*

8   *teenager in the United States. Alex struggles to make sense of*

9   *his experience to her — searching for words, bursting out with*

10   *the most fearful recollection of his father being abducted, his*

11   *mother's pitiful health, and above all the pressure he feels at*

12   *being the only "man" in the family, with so much expected*

13   *of him.)*

14

15   I want to go. I want to go so much, just for one night. I

16   want to leave my sister and the sound of my mother's

17   rattled breathing and the fact that there is no money

18   and if I could shove everything into a paper bag ... I live

19   in a different world. In my dreams my father is taken

20   from us night after night. I could help him, I'm right

21   there, but I'm rooted to the ground. And he is taken

22   night after night. In my dreams I cannot reach my

23   mama's medicine. It's just beyond my fingers and I

24   reach and reach and she chokes to death right in front

25   of me. When I awake, sometimes I forget. I go to school

26   and hear conversations about homework. I hear music.

27   Friends shouting to each other from opposite ends of

28   the hallway. The noise is so comforting. I forget and I

29   want to talk about homework and I start to have fun. I

1   cannot have fun. As soon as my sister gets home from
2   school they run into the kitchen and turn on the taps to
3   see if we have running water. I cannot go to dances. I
4   am the man of the family.
5
6
7
8
9
10
11
12
13
14
15
16
17
18
19
20
21
22
23
24
25
26
27
28
29
30
31
32
33
34
35

Under the Big Top
by Emilio Iasiello

1   Johnny — teens   Male — Serious
2
3   *(Johnny is a young and successful wirewalker in the*
4   *circus. In the following speech he has just been asked by a*
5   *Newspaperman why he does that for an occupation. This is*
6   *a ladder-type of monolog, where the actor must select "high*
7   *emotional points" along the way as Johnny describes the*
8   *important incident that motivated him to join the circus. The*
9   *piece is rich in emotional colors: the fantasy of Johnny's*
10   *delight when high in the air, the curiosity he expresses while*
11   *he nostalgically recollects the incident from his boyhood, his*
12   *contempt and respect for the crowds who both hope and fear*
13   *that he will fall, and his pride in what he does — to mention*
14   *only a few. And in the "acting-out" sections indicated by the*
15   *stage directions, the actor can vividly physicalize both the sense*
16   *of the words and the character's inner emotional condition.)*
17
18   When you still believe in things, you trust in yourself.
19   You accept things more. You don't question the reasons
20   behind it. You just do it. I did it. That's why I made it
21   where I am now. That's how I got away from the
22   neighborhood. I believed, end of story. *(HE looks hard at*
23   *the Newspaperman.)* The thing about stories is that one
24   is just as good as another. It's in the telling that counts.
25   So I'm going to say how it happened. Like I remember.
26   And you draw your own conclusions. So why I was out
27   in the street isn't so important as the fact that I was
28   there. Looking up at this man, this little man, walking
29   between two buildings on a strip of wire. A strip of wire,

can you believe it? You had to see him — this dark
imprint inching across the sky. It was fantastic. *(As HE*
recollects, HE starts to walk in a straight line, putting one foot
in front of the other as if walking on a wire.) Which isn't to
say everyone liked it. Gawking up at this fool, with — I
don't know, is jealousy the right word? Envy? Mistrust?
They wanted him to fall. They dared him to. They
expected to see it happen. And why not? Who bumps
his head against convention? So they ridiculed him.
They shouted his name like a swear. They shook their
fists ... See, idolatry is a dangerous thing. It's a double-
edged sword. The crowd wanted to see themselves in
this man, but they couldn't. He was too much above
them for that. So if they couldn't soar with him, they
would settle to see him fail. *(A slight smile:)* But he didn't.
He wasn't going to. None of them realized that. It wasn't
about falling. There was more to it than that. Something
that their narrow visions couldn't understand. He was
above them all — the streets and the newspapers and
the filth. Above the car horns and insults. I was just a
kid then, ten tops. But even I recognized it for what it
was. Being a king for a minute is still a king. *(JOHNNY*
walks as if on a wire, arms outstretched.) And then, almost
on a whim, he did a dip. *(JOHNNY dips.)* Hundreds of feet
in the air, and this man dips. Right there, he just gets
down on one knee. And then you should have heard
them. Dead silence. Not one peep. No one said a thing.
(JOHNNY smiles.) Thief, cop, businessman, everyone —
stood with their eyes popping out of their heads. And
this man, this wirewalker stopped the pulse of an entire
city. It was the most amazing thing ... *(HE stops walking,*
turns back to Newspaperman.) So to answer your
question, that's when I knew it. I wanted to touch the
sky, walk on clouds. To struggle against failure and
danger. What better way to live, than in the air?

Fishing the Moon
by Scott McMorrow

1	Young Man — teens	Male — Serious

2

3   *(This is a climactic speech, with the peak of emotional*
4   *intensity occurring close to the very end. It is somewhat*
5   *unusual, however, because the Young Man's tale is strongly*
6   *colored by his recollection of the incident and his emotional*
7   *need to distance himself from the painful emotions by*
8   *dampening the experience in recounting it. The actor must*
9   *therefore be careful to avoid delivering the speech as a*
10   *"memory piece," containing little emotional involvement in*
11   *the narration. A second interesting feature for the actor to play*
12   *is the Young Man's repeated attempts to avoid discussing the*
13   *incident by seizing upon any occasion to "parade his*
14   *knowledge" of sea conditions, the emergency drill followed*
15   *by the crew, the "funny thing" of how boats behave in the*
16   *waves, etc. The piece becomes most engaging when the*
17   *auditors can sense the powerful fear underlying the Young*
18   *Man's story.)*

19

20   **The storm hit in the blackness of night. Wind and waves**
21   **roaring and slamming the boat like a wild beast. All I**
22   **could do was turn the bow straight into the worst of it.**
23   **We didn't want to take one broadside. They say you can**
24   **tell where you are in a wave by the color of the thing.**
25   **Clear and foamy puts you near the top. When you look**
26   **out the wheelhouse and see green then you're**
27   **somewhere in the middle. If you're staring into dark, the**
28   **boat is at the base of the thing and it's most likely time**
29   **to go to Jesus. Course, for us, it was night, now wasn't**

1   it. Tough to tell between green and black. One thing was
2   sure, there was nothing clear in sight.
3   Lost the autopilot right off. Had to steer her by hand.
4   The whole crew was up, bouncing around like popcorn.
5   We tied a man, Rick was his name, to the wheel just so
6   he could keep both hands on it. Next thing we knew a
7   monster wave smashed into the forward window and
8   shattered it. Water was pouring in hard and fast.
9   Everyone was in their survival suits. I had the crew get
10   out the saw. The plan was to cut up the galley table and
11   plug the broken window. The ropes we tied around
12   Rick's wrists were cutting into him hard, drawing blood.
13   Poor soul never got time to complain. Another huge
14   wave crested over the bow and nailed him square in the
15   chest. Blew him right through the side of the
16   wheelhouse and into the churning sea. The plan
17   changed in a heartbeat. I had the boys tie themselves
18   together by running a rope around their waists while I
19   turned the boat. Took a couple broadside that almost
20   put us under. We got the spotlight on Rick. He was
21   bobbing up and down like a cork. Each man on deck
22   took up a gaff. I was planning to bring Rick alongside so
23   we could jab the oversized hooks into him. I was yelling
24   not to stick him in any vital organs, just jab him
25   through a shoulder or leg. There they were, lined up on
26   the starboard rail hoping for the chance to impale our
27   crewmate. Funny thing about boats. The V-shape hull
28   means you've got to actually hit the target so it'll run
29   down the side. Rick was about three feet off the bow
30   when a wave rolled the boat. We could all hear him
31   screaming at us as he passed down the opposite side.
32   That was the last we saw of Rick. We still had other fish
33   in the skillet. The ocean was still pouring in through the
34   wheelhouse window. While I kept calling in the May Day
35   the crew formed a bucket brigade to bail the water out.

1   By daybreak the worst of it was over. When the Coast
2   Guard arrived they said it looked like we had been
3   through a war.
4
5
6
7
8
9
10
11
12
13
14
15
16
17
18
19
20
21
22
23
24
25
26
27
28
29
30
31
32
33
34
35

Dear Mother and All
by Sandra Perlman

1   Chet — twenties   Male — Serious

3   *(This monolog is based on an actual letter sent home from a*
4   *young American infantryman during World War One. Its*
5   *structure is noteworthy, because it seems to be the tale of just*
6   *another ordinary day in a soldier's life, when the narrator*
7   *suddenly encounters a familiar face from back home. But the*
8   *joy of reunion and the camaraderie of sharing a meal and a*
9   *few words together, suddenly turns very bleak at the end*
10 *when we learn that the speaker will never see his old friend*
11 *again after this brief encounter. The actor should locate strong*
12 *emotions to play in the monolog. It contains excitement,*
13 *pride, determination, surprise and elation, and finally regret*
14 *and poignant sadness before drawing to a close.)*

16 **The first day of the drive, and our regiment was in that**
17 **first wave. We gained our objective about noon — but it**
18 **took us all afternoon to dig in. Towards evening the**
19 **Germans made a counter-attack — and we drove them**
20 **back again and again. The Huns were dropping '77s all**
21 **around us and sometimes it seemed they would never**
22 **stop coming. Suddenly, it got real quiet. Then the Fifth**
23 **Regiment came up and started digging in right in front**
24 **of us. They were the next ones over the top, all right,**
25 **and they were happy for the rest. We were pretty hungry**
26 **and took the break for chow, when who should I meet**
27 **just then, but Vernon. He was real hungry, too. Hadn't**
28 **eaten a thing all day. Naturally, I gave him part of mine.**
29 **The fortunate thing was just that afternoon I'd found**

1   three whole loaves of that French bread, and so I had
2   one for each of us and one to split again. I gave this
3   whole bread to him and he was so pleased. Wasn't it
4   lucky I had those two extras? So, there we were, in this
5   hole in France, talking about the folks back home and
6   how we were going to tell them all we had gone through.
7   Then Vernon got word to go forward and dig in. So, we
8   shook hands, I wished him good luck and — then he
9   disappeared. Funny, I still had his extra half in my
10   hands.
11
12
13
14
15
16
17
18
19
20
21
22
23
24
25
26
27
28
29
30
31
32
33
34
35

This Phone Will Explode at the Tone

by Lindsay Price

1 Harry — 15   Male — Comic

2

3 *(This comic speech gives the actor ample opportunity to*

4 *physicalize Harry's tense emotions throughout the entirety of*

5 *the monolog. One of the unusual challenges of the piece is*

6 *the fact that the tension never lets up: most of the humor*

7 *derives from the sight of Harry struggling with panic from*

8 *beginning to end. And the conclusion gives the actor a large*

9 *number of choices in how to play the final line.)*

10

11 Hi, Anne? This is Harry. That's right, Harry! I was

12 wondering if you'd like to go out on Friday night. Catch

13 a movie? You would? That's great. I'll pick you up at

14 seven, babe. Bye! Now. All I have to do is actually dial

15 her number and I'll have this down pat. Although ... I've

16 asked the dial tone out so many times maybe she'll go

17 out with me. Hi, everyone — this is my date: the dial

18 tone. Okay. I can do this. I'll just take some deep

19 breaths and pick up the phone and call her. It's just a

20 phone! It's easy. Millions of guys do it every day. I mean,

21 the population would seriously decrease if guys didn't

22 ask girls out on dates. And vice-versa. Oh, jeez, I could

23 get into trouble over that. What if she thinks I'm a sexist

24 pig because I want to ask her out on a date? I'm much

25 too young for this. At least I don't have to see her face

26 when she rejects me. This way she can politely turn me

27 down, we can both hang up and I will quietly bang the

1   receiver against my head all night. Pick up the phone.
2   Pick up the phone. AHHHHH!! What is the worst she can
3   say? She can say no. Would that be so bad? It would be
4   so bad. It would ruin my very existence. As little
5   existence as I have ... it would ruin it completely. Okay.
6   Okay. Maybe some pushups. I'll do some pushups and
7   get the blood running to my head. Yeah! Hello, Anne, will
8   you go out with me? If you need some convincing feel my
9   manly arms! I do a hundred pushups every day! Or
10   maybe two. Enough, enough, enough! It's probably busy.
11   That would solve all my problems. That's it. It's busy.
12   She's probably not even home. I could leave a message.
13   I don't even have to talk to her! I have nothing to worry
14   about. I'm picking up the phone! I'm dialing her number!
15   I'm ... oh my God — it's ringing!
16
17
18
19
20
21
22
23
24
25
26
27
28
29
30
31
32
33
34
35

Too Much Punch for Judy
by Mark Wheeller

1	Duncan Wick — twenties Male — Seriocomic

2

3 *(This is a stepping-stone monolog in which the speaker is*
4 *struggling to come to grips with two problems: the horrific*
5 *experience of having to deal with a fatal auto accident*
6 *outside his home, and the incredulity of its aftermath in his*
7 *life, his local neighborhood, and in society in general. The*
8 *first problem takes a narrative form where the actor must*
9 *describe the experience while re-living it for the audience, so*
10 *that it loses none of its shock value and immediacy. This*
11 *section contains numerous "peaks and valleys" of emotion:*
12 *incredulity, disgust, horror, black humor, and surprise,*
13 *among others. But the second problem the monolog*
14 *addresses is more disturbing for Duncan, because he must*
15 *grapple with the insoluble paradox of the "ordinariness" of*
16 *death, the seeming cheapness of human life, and society's*
17 *seeming indifference to the phenomenon.)*

18

19 I guess it was about midnight and there was one hell of
20 a mighty crash, completely and utterly unannounced by
21 any of the normal sounds that one might associate with
22 a road accident ... Howls of tires, screeching and what
23 have you. I was just mesmerized. I couldn't think what
24 it was and all I could hear was "We've Only Just Begun"
25 by the Carpenters blasting out from what I later
26 discovered to be the car stereo. I got out of bed and
27 looked out of the window. There was a Renault 5 buried
28 in the bridge, just literally sort of disappeared into the
29 bridge parapet. My immediate reaction was "Oh shit! I

1   don't want to be involved in that! I'll let someone else go
2   and have a look." I waited ... maybe half a minute, hoping
3   that someone would get out of the bloody thing ... but
4   nobody did. In the end, I pulled on a pair of trousers a
5   pullover and stupidly nothing else and shot across there.
6   I couldn't approach the car from the passenger side, it
7   was too badly damaged, so went to the driver's door. It
8   wouldn't open. I looked inside. I could see two shapes. I
9   tried the door again. The music was blasting out, like it
10   was sort of force ten on the decibel scale. At that point
11   I suddenly realized that I was standing around in bare
12   feet with a lot of glass about the place which was pretty
13   bloody stupid. I thought, "Well, nobody else is coming
14   out to help!", so I shot back inside, dialed 999, reported
15   the accident ... oh yes ... and put some shoes on!
16   When I went back to the car, which was now smelling
17   of petrol, battery fluid, anti freeze, and there was this
18   dripping and hissing ... I was afraid it might catch fire so,
19   put my leg up onto the back wing and forced the driver's
20   side door open. The music was still blasting out, so the
21   first thing I did was to turn off the power which produced
22   dead silence. I was then confronted with these two
23   forms. I felt for a pulse on the passenger. I couldn't find
24   one. There were no ... no life signs at all.
25   The bridge they'd hit was just these upright concrete
26   pillars with scaffolding pipes coming through them. One
27   of these pipes had been bent, and come straight in
28   through the windscreen, missed the driver ... but it was
29   such that the passenger had to have been hit by it. Her
30   head was in a position where it had obviously been
31   thrown back by the force of this pole coming in ... directly
32   on ... to her face. I was sufficiently squeamish not to
33   investigate that one any further. Thank Christ it wasn't
34   bloody daylight, that's all I can say. I remember thinking
35   ... the passenger was either dead or alive. If she's dead,

1   well I can't do anything about it, but what if she starts

2   to wake up, with hideous bloody injuries requiring some

3   attention, what the bloody hell am I to do then? I've done

4   my bit of first aid, but this was way, way, way beyond

5   that ... or anything I'd experienced in my life. That's the

6   frightening thing about it. The fact that she was dead ...

7   was a bloody blessing! *(HE goes to Judy.)*

8   By this time the driver had begun to make signs of

9   recovery, so I managed to find the buckles of her seat

10   belt and release her. "Right, let's get you out of here."

11   She was like a sort of bendy toy really ... I soon realized

12   that she was smashed out of her skull ... drunk. I

13   thought she was going to get so hysterical that I just

14   wouldn't be able to cope, but she didn't actually; she

15   just seemed to go limpish and start to cry.

16   When I got back home I poured myself a great

17   big bloody drink! I opened the curtains and stood

18   and watched the proceedings ... just out of morbid

19   curiosity ... I'm afraid that's inherent in all of us in those

20   kinds of circumstances. I remember feeling slightly

21   angry that so many people in the houses that faced onto

22   it had obviously decided that they didn't want to become

23   involved ... it's just a silly sort of reaction you get in a

24   state of stress ... cos I do understand why ... but bloody

25   muggins here ... why did I have to go out and get

26   involved? I didn't sleep at all. The realization that you've

27   come right next to an extremely violent death was a very

28   unnerving and shattering experience ... and it was

29   annoying. This bloody woman who drove this bloody car

30   hadn't even touched the brakes ... well she couldn't

31   have done! There wasn't a skid mark on the road

32   anywhere! She was that drunk. She didn't even know

33   that she'd gone up the curb, along the pavement and

34   into the parapet ... she was that drunk!

35   I've recently been reading "The Shooting of

1   President Kennedy." He was apparently lying in the
2   hospital after he died and the hospital was returning to
3   normal. There was a comment made that next door two
4   janitors — auxiliaries — were laughing ... laughing over
5   a joke. There was this hollow laughter going down the
6   corridor with a dead president there ... a very harsh
7   irony, eh?
8   Well, a similar thing happened in this situation. The
9   ambulance had gone and you were left with the "roadies"
10   trying to drag the car off the bridge parapet. They were
11   laughing and I thought ... that can't be right. My final
12   reaction was the following morning. I went out there and
13   "society" had cleared up the mess. "Society" had come
14   along with her backup force and cleaned up the mess,
15   and there was not a single sight there, apart from this
16   twisted parapet, and bits and pieces of the car in the
17   brook ... but someone had actually died there. You
18   know ... the ambulance had taken away the broken
19   body ... and the mortuary had taken care of it from then
20   on. There wasn't any blood ... there wasn't anything. The
21   place had been sanitized. It was an extraordinary
22   sensation, and yet a human life had disappeared there,
23   and you felt ... well, I felt that there should be something
24   there that actually proved the point ... but there was
25   nothing.
26
27
28
29
30
31
32
33
34
35

A List for Reb Pinchas
by Sandra Fenichel Asher

1   Storyteller — Indeterminate Age   Male — Comic
2
3   *(This extended monolog is a complete story. In fact, the*
4   *character is the Storyteller himself from a full-length play. It*
5   *derives from the storytelling tradition in Jewish culture, and*
6   *is an excellent example of "Jewish humor." The actor will*
7   *find numerous words and Yiddish phrases that are necessary*
8   *to understand and may not be changed because they capture*
9   *so brilliantly the personality of the teller and the culture he's*
10   *describing. Of particular interest here is the actor's need to*
11   *impersonate the voices of the other characters described in*
12   *the piece — an acting challenge essential for an effective*
13   *performance. And when the tale is performed well, the*
14   *personality of the Storyteller will emerge as the most*
15   *compelling centerpiece of the whole experience.)*
16
17   **When the earth was created and the time came to fill it**
18   **with people, two angels were chosen and each was given**
19   **a sack: one filled with wise souls and the other with**
20   **foolish souls. The idea was to sprinkle wise and foolish**
21   **souls evenly over the earth, but — ooooops, whooops!**
22   **The angel carrying the sack of foolish souls tripped over**
23   **a mountain peak, and the entire sack of fools spilled**
24   **out! Nitwits, noodlebrains, and pudding-heads tumbled**
25   **from the heavens. Schlemiels, schlemazels, and**
26   **dumkops of every kind landed in one spot — one tiny**
27   **shtetl — one ridiculous speck of a town made up**
28   **entirely of fools — Chelm! Of course, the people of**
29   **Chelm did not know they were fools, for no one who was**

1   from there could tell them. And no one who was not from
2   there could convince them. So — who are we to break
3   such news? They simply believed that, for no particular
4   reason, foolish things were always happening to them.
5   Take, for instance, Pinchas: a rebbe, a teacher, an
6   intellectual. But not so practical. One morning he came
7   running to Reb Mottel, the mayor — a practical man, but
8   in a Chelmish sort of way. *(As Pinchas:)* "Reb Mottel! I
9   must speak to you privately for a moment. I am a deeply
10   troubled man. A terrifying thing has happened to me.
11   Ssssh! Come closer. I don't want the others to hear. This
12   morning, this very morning, I heard the cock crowing and
13   I jumped out of bed. And suddenly I found myself
14   whirling and twirling, this way and that. 'Oi, vay iss mer!
15   A catastrophe! A disaster! What to do?' I called to my
16   wife, 'Rifke! Help me!' My poor wife rushed to my side.
17   *(As Rifke:)* 'My darling Pinchas, what is it? What's wrong?
18   Are you ill?' *(As Pinchas:)* 'No, no, I'm not ill. Listen to
19   me, Rifke, please. I have just awakened from a long
20   night's sleep — and I do not remember where I put my
21   clothes before going to bed!' *(As Rifke:)* 'Dumkop!' she
22   screamed, right in my face. 'If you'll look for once with
23   your eyes open and your mouth shut, maybe you'll see
24   something for a change. Your clothes are right in front of
25   your nose!' *(As Pinchas:)* Right in front of my nose! Reb
26   Mottel, I ask you, how could I forget a thing like that? My
27   nose is always here, and the front of it is always there,
28   and — *(As Mottel:)* "Reb Pinchas, you should know what
29   the good people of Chelm always say: Your absent-
30   mindedness only proves what a wise man you are. With
31   a head so filled with glorious thoughts, should you be
32   bothered to remember trivial details?" *(As Storyteller:)*
33   Then Reb Mottel offered Reb Pinchas a brilliant solution
34   to his problem. *(As Mottel:)* "I suggest you make a list.
35   Tonight as you get undressed and put your clothes away,

1 write down where each and every item goes. Tomorrow
2 morning, when you wake up, all you have to do is follow
3 your list." *(As Pinchas:)* "A list! I'll do it! A list!" *(As*
4 *Storyteller:)* And that night, as he got ready for bed, Reb
5 Pinchas made himself a list. *(As Pinchas, writing each*
6 *item down as he says it:)* "My coat I hang up on a peg,
7 like so. Coat ... on ... peg. My boots I place under the
8 bed, like so. Boots ... under ... bed. So! My shirt I drape
9 on the bedpost, like so. Shirt ... on ... bedpost. So! My
10 talis I fold up neat, like so. Talis ... neatly ... folded ...
11 so! My hat on the other post, like so. Hat ... on ... post.
12 So! And myself I put into the bed, like so. I ... am ... in ...
13 bed. So! A list! Good night." *(As Storyteller:)* The next
14 morning, Reb Pinchas awoke with the cock's crow and
15 to his great joy, he still held the list tightly in his hand.
16 *(As Pinchas:)* "Aha! My list. Now we're in business. Let
17 me see. Coat ... on ... peg. So! My coat I hung from a
18 peg. Like so! Boots ... under ... bed. So! My boots I
19 placed under the bed. Like so! Trousers ... over ... chair,
20 so! My trousers went over the chair. Like so! Shirt ...
21 on ... bedpost. So! My shirt I draped over the bedpost.
22 Like so! Talis ... neatly folded. So! My talis I folded up
23 neat. Like so! Hat ... on ... post. So! My hat's on the
24 other post. Like so! Everything right in front of my nose!
25 *(HE reads another item on his list:)* What's this? One more
26 item on my list? I ... am ... in ... bed. *(HE checks bed:)*
27 But I am not in bed! Oi vay! I'm gone! Rifke, help!" *(As*
28 *Rifke:)* "What is it, Pinchas? What's wrong? Are you
29 hurt?" *(As Pinchas:)* "No, I am not hurt. I am gone!" *(As*
30 *Rifke:)* "Gone? Gone where?" *(As Pinchas:)* "How should
31 I know where? I'm gone. I'm a missing person!" *(As*
32 *Rifke:)* "A missing person, now?" said Rifke. "A dumkop,
33 you mean! What did I do to deserve such craziness in
34 my house? Close the windows, the neighbors shouldn't
35 hear." *(As Pinchas:)* "No! No! Open the windows! Rifke!

1   Someone! Anyone! Help me ... wherever I am!" *(As*
2   *Storyteller:)* **And did Reb Pinchas receive help at last? Of**
3   **course. It was Gimpel the fool who finally found him.** *(As*
4   *Gimpel:)* **"You know, Reb Pinchas, what is not in the bed**
5   **has often fallen under the bed."** *(As Storyteller:)* **And**
6   **under the bed went Pinchas to begin his search.** *(As*
7   *Gimpel:)* **"Reb Pinchas? Reb Pinchas, where are you?"**
8   *(As Pinchas:)* **"I'm under the bed, Gimpel."** *(As Storyteller:)*
9   **And under the bed went Gimpel.** *(As Gimpel:)* **"Ah! So**
10   **here you are! Just as I suspected."** *(As Pinchas:)* **"So**
11   **here I am! I'm under the bed! I'm found! It's a miracle!"**
12   *(As Storyteller:)* **A miracle! What can I tell you? When**
13   **you are a wise man of Chelm, miracles — like foolish**
14   **things — happen every day!**
15
16
17
18
19
20
21
22
23
24
25
26
27
28
29
30
31
32
33
34
35

Heading West
by Philip Goulding

1   Dare Bryan — twenties   Male — Serious
2
3   *(The following selection takes the form of a stepping-stone*
4   *speech, where Dare Bryan chronicles abuses that he and his*
5   *fellow emigrants have suffered on the voyage. The speech*
6   *increases in intensity, however, as Dare Bryan becomes*
7   *increasingly nervous and uncomfortable, fearing how his*
8   *words are being received by the Captain. This poses a wealth*
9   *of choices for the actor to identify those parts of the speech*
10   *where Dare Bryan might encounter strong reactions from the*
11   *Captain — to "score" the speech with emotional responses of*
12   *Dare Bryan and his listener: fear, hostility, impatience,*
13   *assertiveness, threat, etc. Of special note here is the way in*
14   *which the actor chooses to play the ending: is Dare Bryan*
15   *confident? wary? courageous? questioning? Which is the*
16   *most effective?)*
17
18   I have here a petition ... a document if you will ... (as
19   due to the recent adverse conditions I was unable to
20   obtain as many signatures as I had intended) ... oh, and
21   I would also like it noted that some passengers actually
22   declined to sign this paper for fear of being violently
23   interfered with by certain officers under your command.
24   However ... call it letter, call it list, call it what you like,
25   you'll find my complaints and reservations as to the
26   conditions on this vessel clearly set down here in
27   black and white. *(HE reads:)* "Respected Sir, We, the
28   undersigned passengers on board the ship the Western
29   Queen paid for and secured our passages in her in the

1   confident expectation that the allowance of provisions
2   promised us in our contract tickets would be faithfully
3   delivered to us. I must report, however, that this has not
4   always been the case. On a number of occasions water
5   provisions have been withheld from certain passengers,
6   and when I have made attempt to query these decisions
7   with the First Mate — Mr. Shavitz — he has berated me
8   using blasphemous and abusive language, save on one
9   occasion when he actually dispensed with such
10   pleasantries, and instead simply knocked me to the
11   ground. In the matter of other provisions I admit that I
12   personally have received more than my due in flour, and
13   most of my due in sugar, but I have thus far only
14   received half my allowance of biscuits, rice, oatmeal and
15   tea. I have received no pork, and only a third of my
16   molasses. It also merits mention that passengers' food
17   is seldom cooked sufficiently, due to a deficiency of
18   stoves." Might I also take this opportunity to remind the
19   Captain of the Order of Council made by the emigration
20   commissioners in 1848, which laid down, amongst
21   others, the following rules for conduct: "Rule 6: All decks
22   to be dry holystoned or scraped at nine o'clock in the
23   morning. Rule 14: All passengers to be assembled in
24   clean linen and decent apparel at half-past ten on
25   Sundays. Rule 21: Swearing and improper language
26   strictly forbidden." *(Pause.)* I'm afraid we now come to
27   the section where I ... that is ... we address yourself in
28   particular, sir. "We would also like it documented here
29   that the Captain never appears to trouble himself in the
30   slightest degree about the passengers, nor ever visit any
31   part of the ship occupied by them. No one knows of the
32   whereabouts of the vessel except the Captain and first
33   mate and they keep that information a profound secret
34   from the ship's company and passengers ... "
35

Histrionica with Banjo
by Brian Torrey Scott

1 Gregory — Indeterminate Age   Male — Comic
2
3 *(This is a climactic monolog, although the actual point in the*
4 *monolog where the climax is reached poses several possibilities*
5 *for the actor to play. Additionally, Gregory's mood also permits*
6 *a wide variety of interpretation. Is he genuinely struggling*
7 *with a profound existential question of his own identity? Or*
8 *is he merely wallowing in trivia while waiting for the*
9 *waitress to bring his meal? The actor should in any case*
10 *avoid making the un-dramatic choice that Gregory is "simply*
11 *bored." He is obviously obsessed by something that he can't*
12 *explain — whether it be his own perceptions, the alienation*
13 *he observes in society, the frustration with his job, or some*
14 *other frustrating problem. The important thing is for the actor*
15 *to "find Gregory's itch that he simply must scratch" in order*
16 *to play the monolog effectively.)*
17
18 **Some things were really bothering me the other night**
19 **while I was eating. Have you ever noticed how every**
20 **person's actions change depending on who they are with**
21 **and where they are? Seriously, I have never thought**
22 **about that. But I was eating. Alone. I guess I never eat**
23 **alone. I got to thinking. The waitress brings me water**
24 **and a menu. That's the first part. She seemed to have**
25 **a whole routine planned out for me. For every customer.**
26 **She slides into my space, yet she is completely**
27 **impersonal. She is a robot. "The specials of the day are**
28 **... ?" She left and I really just tried to forget about it. I**
29 **was hungry. I look out the window and I see all these**

1   people walking by, and they're all not thinking about
2   each other or the waitress or me. That actually
3   comforted me. For them not to think about me. To see
4   me. They just swim by like fish and I watch. Then I
5   noticed that I was thinking about them. Do they choose
6   not to think about me? The waitress won't notice me in
7   a crowd tomorrow. And I wouldn't notice her. Now I
8   would. The problem is ... well, what's bothering me
9   about that is that I felt comfortable not being thought
10   about but I felt good thinking about other people. Am I
11   complicating their lives? Am I intruding an extra element
12   into reality? I realize that everything we do is like that.
13   We keep adding more and more on top of more and
14   more. I am born. I grow up. Now I need to support myself
15   so I go to school. I go to school so now I am going to get
16   a job. My specialties allow me into a small office full of
17   files and computers where there is even more to add.
18   Things that I didn't even learn in school ... *(Pause.)* Of
19   course, I'm not talking about me, but them. The fish.
20
21
22
23
24
25
26
27
28
29
30
31
32
33
34
35

Visiting
by Evan Guilford-Blake

1	Zhen — 19 Male — Serious

1   Zhen — 19   Male — Serious

2

3   *(This monolog springs from Zhen's overpowering desire to*

4   *share with another listener his experience of visiting his*

5   *grandmother's grave. Although it begins ordinarily enough,*

6   *the first part of the piece must be infused with the same*

7   *enthusiasm that Zhen brings to the second part — the day is*

8   *too perfect, the clouds too white, the birds and butterflies too*

9   *carefree, and so on. As Zhen's excitement builds to the very*

10 *end, we begin to suspect that this is more than just a story that*

11 *happened in the past: it is a profoundly moving experience that*

12 *infuses the character's present life as well. The actor must*

13 *present the story with a great deal of "honesty" — overt*

14 *theatricality should be avoided. The piece moves from ordinary*

15 *storytelling through moments of curiosity and humor, surprise*

16 *and discovery, to the final moments, of confidence and joy.)*

17

18 **Last Sunday was my grandmother's birthday. I went out**

19 **to visit her — drove; the first time Dad'd let me take the**

20 **car to go anywhere outside the city — I just got my**

21 **license a few weeks ago; I had to wait 'cause I was —**

22 **sick the last couple of years.**

23   **It's not that far, maybe forty miles; just a little past**

24 **"civilization," just into the country. It's a pretty drive on**

25 **a nice day, and Sunday was beautiful. The trees'd just**

26 **budded, there were those little yellow flowers, I don't**

27 **know what they're called but they smelled wonderful, all**

28 **along the roadside. Just enough breeze so it was**

29 **comfortable to ride with the window open and listen to**

1   the whip of the wind 'nstead of the air conditioner. Not
2   a lot of traffic, which surprised me. But maybe that was
3   because I left early. The sky was very blue. Nimbus
4   clouds, lots of birds. Butterflies and birds.
5   I got there about ten o'clock, right when they
6   opened. I parked in the lot and walked; it's kind of a long
7   way — we're on the west side; it's the oldest part, some
8   of the stones go back to the 1800s. They had a farm
9   near there, my grandparents; a really successful one. I
10   laid the flowers I brought on her grave, and then I just
11   stood there a while. It was so quiet. Grandpa was the
12   one who bought all the plots — 96 of them! — so we
13   could be buried together, at least for a few generations.
14   And they're all marked — we all know where we're going
15   to spend eternity. Where our bodies will, anyway. Mine is
16   near the southern edge, right under a tree. I could see it
17   from Grandma's, the tree, and, and standing there?,
18   looking on it, I could imagine — no; no, not imagine: I
19   realized I knew what it was like, to lie there, in the earth,
20   to not know and, and yet to know: That there was a
21   world you'd been a part of, full of sadness and loss, and
22   laughter and love. I felt — I felt, for a minute, like I did
23   when I was in the hospital. I dreamed, in the coma. I
24   know I did, even if I can't remember them. But I knew —
25   something; when I woke up, I knew there was a world —
26   one where sight and sound and smell — didn't matter —
27   a world — apart, from this one, and I knew I'd been a
28   part of it, too. And even if I tried I would never be able
29   not to know that. It's funny — when I woke up, the first
30   thing I did?, was cry.
31   Anyway, I stood there, looking even though I think
32   my eyes were closed. Then I kissed Grandma — her
33   stone I mean — and I walked back. I didn't stop at my
34   plot, or at any of the other graves. I'll come out here
35   again; there's plenty of time.

The Government Inspector
by Nickolai Gogol,
new version by Philip Goulding

1 Petty — twenties   Male — Comic
2
3 *(John Petty is visiting a small provincial town and has been*
4 *mistaken for an important government inspector. Playing the*
5 *charade to the hilt, Petty impresses the locals at every turn.*
6 *In the following speech, he has been drinking steadily*
7 *throughout the day and is now "in his cups." The actor*
8 *should remember that the man is not "drunk," and that the*
9 *most effective way of playing intoxication onstage is to take*
10 *your model from life: an intoxicated person does not try to act*
11 *intoxicated, but instead struggles to appear sober. This*
12 *stepping-stone speech has been removed from its Russian*
13 *setting and relocated to Great Britain by its English*
14 *translator.)*
15
16 *(Admiring the mayor's wife:)* **Ah, but the country! Its**
17 **fascinating undulations. Its rising hills and dappled**
18 **brooks. Its sweetly scented dappled valleys. These are**
19 **charms that can't compare.** *(HE snaps out of it and starts*
20 *to play the room.)* **Oh, the city, I grant you, teems with**
21 **life. "Cest la veeay," as we say chez noose. You see, you**
22 **might well imagine me some lowly pen-pusher. Not so!**
23 **I'm on very good terms with the head of my department.**
24 **Many's the time he claps me on the shoulder like so,**
25 **and cries: "Come to dinner, dear boy, we'd so love to**
26 **have you!" Suffice to say, I try to put my face round the**
27 **office door at least once a day. Put them straight on**
28 **certain complicated clerical matters. And then there's**

1   the poor copying clerk, scratching and scribbling away.
2   Just writes my letters for me. All day, every day. Head
3   down. Scribble scribble scribble. Scratch scratch
4   scratch. Poor sap. But why is everyone standing? Rank!
5   Rank, indeed. Such things mean little to me. Sit! Good
6   heavens, when did I ever think of rank? I make it my
7   business to pass unnoticed. Incognito. Easier said than
8   done, I grant you. Wherever I go word soon seems to get
9   around. Then, of course, it's a matter of time. "Hey!
10 There's John Petty! It's John Petty. Hey!" I remember I
11 was once mistaken for the Commander-in-Chief himself.
12 Blow me down if nearly the entire army didn't come
13 tumbling out of the guardhouse, saluting and presenting
14 arms like nobody's business! How they ... laughed —
15 when they realized their error. And, of course, I'm friends
16 with all the prettiest young actresses. Having dabbled
17 myself with knocking off a few trifles for the stage. Oh
18 yes, I move in distinctly literary circles. Dickens is a
19 great pal of mine. "Dickie," I say. "How's tricks, Dick?"
20 "So-so, old chap," says he. "Musn't grumble." He's very
21 humble. And of course, I write a bit myself. Oh, yes,
22 "The Marriage of Figaro," "The Origin of Species,"
23 "Much Ado About Nothing" ... I can't remember all the
24 titles. I didn't intend to write for the theatre at all but
25 this chap from Drury Lane absolutely insisted. He's
26 always coming to me, cap in hand, when attendances
27 are down. So I dash off another one to keep the place
28 going. The last effort took me an entire evening. Art can
29 be a cruel master. Some of us have been blessed with
30 the gift to speak from our souls, some haven't.
31 Literature's my life blood, nothing less! I host the best
32 respected salon in the city. Everyone knows it. Strangers
33 point as they pass. "That's John Petty's place," they cry.
34 I say, if you're ever in the city, I trust you'll all honor me
35 with your presence. My balls are the talk of the town.

1   Taste, of course, is the key. As the centerpiece, a huge
2   watermelon. I won't bore you with the cost of such a
3   thing. A thousand pounds at least. The soup I have
4   imported, directly from Par-ee. In special tureens. You
5   lift the lids and ... ! That aroma! It'd bring you to your
6   knees. We dance all night, and when we're tired of
7   that ... there's always whist. It's a pretty exclusive club,
8   of course. The Foreign Minister himself, the French
9   Ambassador, the German Foreign Minister, and me. It's
10   quite exhausting keeping up. Though languages are my
11   specialty. *(HE might attempt to demonstrate this.)* **Anyway,**
12   by the time I get home I can hardly make it up those
13   four flights of stairs to my flat. My major-domo
14   stumbles out of the kitchen and I cry ... *(Seeking*
15   *inspiration:)* "Sidebottom! Quick as you can! Take my
16   coat, there's a good man!" *(Pause.)* **Wait a minute. What**
17   am I saying? What absolute nonsense. *(Pause.)* **Forgive**
18   me ... I'm forgetting. *(Pause.)* **Of course, I live on the first**
19   floor. Ah, but if you could peep into that fabulous
20   reception room early in the morning, before I'm even up
21   and out. Princes and Counts, buzzing about. Like bees
22   around a honey pot. Moths to a flame. Sometimes even
23   the Prime Minister drops by. And my letters, of course,
24   come addressed to "His Excellency." I remember once I
25   had to take charge of the entire department. The
26   Director had disappeared for some reason, mysteriously,
27   no one knew where. There was a great deal of talk as to
28   who should take his place. Some of our great Generals
29   tried to fill the post, but it was hopeless, one after
30   another they had to admit defeat. So the task naturally
31   fell to me. A complete surprise, of course. I went out on
32   to my balcony one morning to find crowds of
33   messengers in the street. Thirty-five ... thousand at
34   least! A cry went up — "Your country needs you!" At
35   first I thought it polite to refuse. Out of modesty. But

1	come lunch time public order was threatened, so I had
2	to reluctantly concede. After all, if it reached the ears of
3	Her Majesty, heaven knows what the outcome might be.
4	"But I must warn you," I said. "There will be changes
5	at every level! No stone will remain unturned in my
6	search for inefficiency and corruption!" That stirred
7	them up, I can tell you. Like an earthquake it was. Every
8	man among them shook. Like leaves. "There is a new
9	power in the land!" I told them. "I am ubiquitous. I am
10	omnipotent! I've an open invitation to the Palace! I
11	am everywhere! And what's more ... tomorrow ... I shall
12	be ... Field-Marshal!"
13	
14	
15	
16	
17	
18	
19	
20	
21	
22	
23	
24	
25	
26	
27	
28	
29	
30	
31	
32	
33	
34	
35	

Five Days to Friday
by John Pinckard

1 Dustin — 17   Male — Comic
2
3 *(The amorphous shape of this monolog is truly a challenge*
4 *that presents the actor with numerous possibilities for*
5 *interpretation and for relating directly to the audience. It is*
6 *best played with the audience as the vis-à-vis, instead of an*
7 *imaginary listener. Despite its apparent lack of focus,*
8 *however, it does lead from a beginning, through a middle, to*
9 *an end. It may not be profound, but it permits a quality of*
10 *absolute authenticity to emerge very strongly from a well-*
11 *prepared actor.)*
12
13 *(HE notices the audience.)* **Whoo! Cool, cool, cool. What?**
14 **Uh-oh, you probably shouldn't be seeing this. Cuz you**
15 **know I probably shouldn't be doing this. Oh well! Sucks,**
16 **huh? I mean, here I am misrepresenting, like a whole,**
17 **you know, dude, man, thing, like demagogic, what,**
18 **pedagogic, no, synagogic, dammit, like, what's that**
19 **thing when it's like a bunch of people? Demographic!**
20 **Like, the party. Like, this party, man, kickin'! I think.**
21 **Whatever. So what was I saying? Like, people, and**
22 **something. Like, you know, when people do stuff, and**
23 **like, you don't want to know about it? And when they**
24 **like tell you anyway, and you get like madder at the**
25 **people for telling you about it than you do about the**
26 **actual doing of it, the thing you don't want to know**
27 **about? Doesn't change whether or not they're doing it.**
28 **The thing, I mean. So we're like partying, and stuff, and**
29 **everyone's like, oh crap, I hope we don't get busted, and**

1   I'm like, oh crap, I hope I don't care! Cuz like what's the
2   point? I don't know. If I knew what the point was I would
3   probably not be here. But I am here, so that's what I am.
4   Here. And pointless. You know, there's a whole bunch of
5   stuff that's pointless. Not just me. Like, velcro. Seating
6   charts. Algebra. They're all just tools, man. Tools for the
7   man. Groovy, dig. Okay, so I am — ssshhh! — a little
8   messed up! Oh no! That makes me an irresponsible
9   youth, check, but I can't be responsible for that. See,
10   cuz, like, people are like, stop the kids from doing this,
11   stop the kids from doing that, it's bad, it's bad, it's bad,
12   ba bad bad! Bad! They don't even care why stuff is going
13   on in the first place, it's just one of those things that
14   you don't want to know about! See, what's bad? Like,
15   say you want to get to Seattle, is it bad to head for L.A.?
16   Naw, man, it's just out of the way. You still get there,
17   just later. Deep, huh? And it's all about the drive there.
18   And the Starbucks once you get there, cuz I could totally
19   go for some coffee or some like, what's that stuff, latte,
20   yeah ...
21
22
23
24
25
26
27
28
29
30
31
32
33
34
35

The Alien Hypothesis
by William Borden

1   Larry — teens   Male — Seriocomic

2

3   *(Larry isn't crazy — or is he? If he is, then maybe we all are.*

4   *This strange question underlies his monolog from beginning*

5   *to end. But more than just a comic treatment of the age-old*

6   *question of identity, Larry is also grappling here with the*

7   *problem of loneliness. The selection poses a challenge to the*

8   *actor playing Larry to fully consider each new thought along*

9   *the way and share it with the audience, as Larry pursues his*

10 *questions. It also demands that the actor balance the comedy*

11 *against the real pain that he's feeling as he tries to extract*

12 *answers from the alien Meewom.)*

13

14 **Do you ever feel ... different? Not like everybody else? Oh,**

15 **everybody's unique — I know that: DNA, fingerprints.**

16 **But some people feel at home, whether they're in New**

17 **York or Paris or ... Fargo. They feel like they belong. I**

18 **don't.** *(Pause.)* **I think I'm from outer space. No, listen,**

19 **I'm not crazy. I'm just entertaining hypotheses about**

20 **my feeling different. One hypothesis might be that I am**

21 **actually an alien from another planet, here in the form**

22 **of an earthling, and I'm programmed not to realize this**

23 **so I'll fit in, except the programming didn't work. Or else**

24 **it did work, and I'm programmed to begin to realize**

25 **the truth now, gradually. And at some time I will — I**

26 **hope — receive further instructions. Maybe a manual,**

27 **like you get with your VCR that explains how to set the**

28 **clock and everything.** *(Pause.)* **Maybe we communicate**

29 **telepathically. But that's what crazy people think! That**

1   they're getting instructions from Alpha Centauri —
2   "Go kill," and so on. I wouldn't hurt anybody. After all,
3   people have been nice to me, even though I am from
4   another planet. Or maybe it's another dimension, you
5   know? There's a lot we don't understand. I'm not looking
6   for special privileges or anything. I'm just trying to find
7   an explanation for these questions that keep popping
8   into my head, like, "Who am I?" And "What am I doing
9   here?" I suppose everybody wonders that, don't they?
10   Maybe not. *(Pause.)* Even when I'm with other people who
11   also feel different — you know, you're sitting around late
12   at night discussing deep things, like the meaning of life,
13   and is God a Moslem or a Jew or an atheist, and you
14   think, here's my club! We're all the same, we're all
15   different! Until you realize you're even more different
16   than the other different people. *(Pause.)* I don't think my
17   girl friend's an alien. She feels like she belongs. I should
18   have another alien for a girl friend. But I'm not attracted
19   to other girls. They're too different. *(Pause.)* I've never
20   seen a flying saucer. If I were really an alien, wouldn't
21   they visit me? Just to say, Hi, Larry, how ya doin'? Keep
22   up the good work ... of being different. Well, they're busy.
23   They're out there making crop circles, abducting
24   humans. Still, they could give a fellow a ring now and
25   then. Birthday card, that sort of thing. *(Pause.)* Unless
26   our nature is that we're different. Our essence is
27   difference. But if my essence is being different, why does
28   it bother me to feel different? I mean, I'm used to it and
29   everything, but ... if I were meant to be different — why
30   do I want to belong — to something ... or someone ... ?
31   *(Pause. HE seems to hear something.)* Hello? Yes? It's so
32   good to glip me after all this time and space and
33   dimensionality? It's good to perceive me with all thirty-
34   seven of your senses? Who ARE you? My girl friend? I
35   have a — you're my ALIEN girl friend? Meewom?

1   Forgotten you? Are you kidding? You're ONE of my alien
2   girl friends? How many ... Thirty-seven! Of course,
3   you're my favorite! Well, you know, I have an earth girl
4   friend ... You don't mind? Great. Listen, Meewom, while
5   I have you here, so to speak — what? You're fifty billion
6   parsecs away? It's a great connection. And a hundred
7   and six dimensions? Wow. It's like you're — right inside
8   my head. I'm not crazy, am I? Hearing voices — hearing
9   your voice — it's a beautiful voice, Meewom — wait —
10   I'm getting a little static — that's better. Listen, while I
11   have you here, coming in clear like this — where the
12   heck have you been? You drop me off on this insane
13   planet, you give me no manual, you leave me to fend for
14   myself like some feral child raised by wolves, I look all
15   over for you, or somebody like you ... like me ... I've
16   been lonely. Why am I here? Are there others like me?
17   What is the plan? Is there any meaning to it all? Did you
18   bring the manual? What? You're fading. You're —
19   Meewom! Meewom! I can't hear — Goodbye? No, no.
20   The what? The interdimensionality time-space warp is
21   dissolving ... ? You just got here! Hello? Hello? Meewom!
22   Meewom? *(Silence. Long pause.)* At least there's been
23   contact. At least ... *(Shouting into the universe:)* I still
24   have a lot of questions! *(Pause.)* But at least now I know.
25   I'm not alone. *(Pause.)* Am I?
26
27
28
29
30
31
32
33
34
35

Why Coyotes Won't Kill You
by Nancy Wright

1   Zave — twenties   Native American Male — Serious

2

3   *(The following selection contains a double vis-à-vis: a human*
4   *listener and, at the end, a coyote pup. In the play, Zave is a*
5   *would-be poet and jack-of-all-trades working on an island*
6   *that could become the next Disney World. He's addressing a*
7   *mother grieving over the tragic bombing in Oklahoma City,*
8   *who has rescued a coyote pup. When presenting the piece,*
9   *the actor must above all attune himself to the "storytelling*
10   *mode," as the playwright calls it. But the "cuteness" of the*
11   *story must always rest upon Zave's need to comfort his*
12   *grieving listener, and Zave's knowledge that there is a far*
13   *more profound meaning to the tale than the simple elements*
14   *that the story might suggest.)*

15

16   You don't know the legend of the Blue Coyote, do you?
17   But I bet you watched Roadrunner cartoons when you
18   were a kid. You had to love Wile E. Coyote ... He's the
19   white man's mass media version of Blue Coyote. See,
20   cartoonists know about coyotes. Or at least they know
21   what Native Americans know. Coyote is a trickster.
22   Clever but gullible — and almost indestructible. He gets
23   in trouble because he gets greedy. He wants it all. But
24   somehow he makes the narrowest escape, and lives to
25   dupe and be duped another day. Like Wile E. Sure, real
26   coyotes are a lot smarter than real roadrunners. But —
27   hey — what's funnier than a beeping roadrunner?
28   Coyotes are about as smart as your average poodle, but
29   they're as curious as a cat. Lucky for them, coyotes are

1   fast enough to get out of most scrapes. MOST scrapes.
2   They don't do real well against firearms, though. But
3   Blue Coyote and Wile E. have a lot in common. And they
4   don't need Roadrunner. All they need is an opportunity
5   to play. *(In a storytelling mode:)* Long, long ago, the
6   bluebird was a dusty color. Every time he flew over a
7   stream, he would see himself and feel sad, thinking,
8   "Man, the water and the sky are so blue, and I am so
9   dull." One day, he decided to try diving into the blue
10   water to see if some of that color might come off on him.
11   So he dove and he dove and he dove. And, finally, it
12   happened. The bluebird turned a bright blue. Meanwhile,
13   on the far shore, Coyote was watching all this, thinking,
14   "I'm kinda dull looking myself. Maybe that would work
15   for me." So Coyote started diving, too. He went again
16   and again and again into the deep blue water. What do
17   you know? Lo and behold, Coyote came out an
18   astonishing bright blue — as vivid as the sky above and
19   the stream below. But just then a rabbit ran by, and —
20   without thinking — Coyote took off after him. He wanted
21   to play, man, so he chased the rabbit all through the
22   brush. Soon Coyote was rolling and kicking in the dust
23   and sand, and his cool blue coat was — you guessed
24   it — gone. Coyote was dull brown again. So he went
25   back to the stream and dove and dove until he dyed it
26   blue one more time. But no matter how many times
27   Coyote colored his coat, he was too much of a party
28   animal to keep it blue for long. Coyotes just wanna have
29   fun. That's why I named this guy's daddy Big Blue. And
30   I'm thinking maybe we should name him Blue, too. In
31   his daddy's honor. In honor of his heritage. Yeah. "Blue
32   Too." T-O-O. *(To the Coyote pup:)* Hey, Little One. In the
33   name of your ancestors and mine, I hereby christen you.
34   May you live as long and be as lucky as Wile E. And may
35   your worst enemy be a roadrunner.

The Sister
by Timothy Miller

1   Teddy — 8-15 years-old   Male — Comic

2

3   *(This brief selection probably expresses a common feeling of*
4   *older siblings at the arrival of a new baby in the house. The*
5   *student should avoid presenting the monolog as a series of*
6   *"rambling" thoughts as Teddy speaks, and instead remember*
7   *that Teddy is really wrestling with a problem. This will tend*
8   *to give the delivery more energy, and a sense of urgency and*
9   *development. For maximum effect, the piece should reach a*
10   *climax at the final "punch line.")*

11

12   **Mom came back from the hospital yesterday. It will be**
13   **nice to have some decent food and have the family**
14   **together again, only it isn't like it was before.** *(Pause.*
15   *Ominously:)* **See, she didn't come back alone. She**
16   **brought my brother's new baby sister with her. She isn't**
17   **MY baby sister, that's for sure. I would NEVER have a**
18   **sister — especially one like that! She's bald, for one,**
19   **like Aunt MaryLee. And she's the wrong color. Kinda**
20   **reddish. And she makes horrible noises — from both**
21   **ends! She doesn't sleep when everybody else does, and**
22   **she doesn't smell so good most of the time either. Dad**
23   **seems excited about her, though. But I've seen Dad get**
24   **excited about stuff before and it almost always turns out**
25   **bad. Like, he was REALLY excited about putting in the**
26   **new garage door opener. The next day, he seemed less**
27   **excited about having to replace the whole front of the**
28   **garage with a big tarp. I'm just sure this whole sister**
29   **thing is gonna go just as bad.** *(Pause.)* **I'll give it a couple**

1   more days, let Mom and Dad get over the pride of new
2   ownership, and then I'll put my foot down. She's got to
3   go back. We don't need any more kids around here —
4   the ones we have don't have enough stuff anyway.
5   *(Pause.)* I wonder if the hospital will give us a refund?
6
7
8
9
10
11
12
13
14
15
16
17
18
19
20
21
22
23
24
25
26
27
28
29
30
31
32
33
34
35

About the Authors

Dori Appel is the author of 16 full-length plays, plus 17 one-acts, shorts and monologs, and more than 50 published poems and stories. Her plays have been produced throughout the U.S., as well as internationally, and her poetry and fiction have been featured in dozens of magazines in addition to several well known anthologies. These include *When I Am An Old Woman I Shall Wear Purple* and *The Best Is Yet To Be*, the audio recording of which was a 1997 Grammy finalist. Dori Appel has won the prestigious Oregon Book Award in Drama both in 1998 and 1999: first for FREUD'S GIRLS, a drama in which Freud's secrets are revealed with help from Virginia Woolf and Anais Nin, and most recently for THE LUNATIC WITHIN, a revue-style comedy/drama about everyday oddities and ordinary madness.

Sandra Fenichel Asher's plays have been produced nationwide; nineteen have been published including A WOMAN CALLED TRUTH, THE WISE MEN OF CHELM, ACROSS THE PLAINS, an adaptation of Jane Austen's *EMMA*, and THE WOLF AND ITS SHADOWS. She has been honored with an NEA grant in playwriting, the IUPUI/Bonderman Award, the Joseph Campbell Memorial Award, a Kennedy Center New Visions/New Voices selection, and the Charlotte Chorpenning Award for a distinguished body of work. Sandy is writer-in-residence at Drury University and a member of Dramatists Guild.

Shirley Barrie co-founded and was Associate Director of the Tricycle Theatre in London, England from 1972 to 1984 where she began writing plays for young audiences. In Toronto, she co-founded Straight Stitching Productions in 1989, and won two Chalmers awards and a Dora for STRAIGHT STITCHING and CARRYING THE CALF, both of which have been published. Her one-act, REVELATION, won the Drama Workshop Playwriting Competition in Des Moines, Iowa in 2000.

Evan Guilford-Blake's many produced works include the multiple award-winning NIGHTHAWKS, CEREMONIES OF PRAYER (winner of the 1996 Utah Playfest Competition), the two-character drama SOME UNFINISHED CHAOS, and TRUE MAGIC, an *a capella* Christmas musical farce. He has also had numerous staged and chamber readings by theatres across the United States. His award-winning fiction and poetry (both adult and children's), as well as his journalism, have been published in various local and national publications; and he has created material and performed extensively for children. He is a Resident Playwright at Chicago Dramatists and at API Theatre of Kalamazoo, Michigan.

William Borden is a core alumnus playwright at The Playwrights' Center in Minneapolis, Playwright In Residence with Listening Winds Theatre, Fiction Editor of THE NORTH DAKOTA QUARTERLY, and Chester Fritz Distinguished Professor of English Emeritus at the University of North Dakota. His plays have won 22 national playwriting competitions and have been widely published in such collections as THE BEST STAGE SCENES OF 1998, ONE-ACT PLAYS FOR ACTING STUDENTS, THE PRAGUE REVIEW, and other books and journals. His plays have had over 180 productions in New York, Los Angeles, Canada, Germany, the Actors Theatre of Louisville, and elsewhere. Mr. Borden lives on a lake in northern Minnesota with his wife of 40 years.

Claire Braz-Valentine's plays have been produced coast-to-coast in the United States, and also overseas. She has devoted the majority of her artistic life to working with incarcerated men, women and teenagers, doing theater with the disadvantaged.

Karen Mueller Bryson is a playwright and actress living in Calgary, Alberta, Canada. The most recent productions of her plays include THAZEL HOFSTETTER LIVES HERE (Bank Street Theatre, New York), THE DOCTOR WILL SEE YOU NOW (Stage Works, Tampa, Florida), BUT DOES HE KNOW BOTICELLI? (Cayuga Community College, Auburn, New York), and GOD'S GRACE (Carrollwood Players, Tampa, Florida).

Max Bush's plays have been widely produced on professional, educational and amateur stages across the United States. He earned his M.F.A. from the University of Michigan, and has won numerous awards for his work, including the Distinguished Play Award from the American Alliance for Theatre in Education, and individual artist grants from the Michigan Council for the Arts and the IUPUI National Playwriting competition. His scripts have been performed on such prestigious stages as the Honolulu Youth Theatre, the Kennedy Center, the Goodman Theatre, the Emmy Gifford Theatre, the Nashville Academy Theatre and elsewhere.

Cynthia L. Cooper's plays have been produced in a variety of venues in New York, across the United States, Canada and Europe, including Women's Project and Productions, Wings Theatre, Primary Stages, Theatreworks USA, and the L.A. Women in Theatre festival. Her writing has also appeared in books published by Applause, Papier Mache Press, Smith & Kraus, Heinemann, and Human Kinetics Press. A Jerome Fellow and playwright-in-residence at the Playwrights' Center in Minneapolis for two years, she directed the Women's Playwriting Conference there. Living and working in New York, she has also published a variety of nonfiction books and articles, in addition to plays. She is a member of the Dramatists Guild and The Authors League.

Sandra Dempsey is a Canadian-Irish playwright who has seen her award-winning plays produced and published throughout Canada, the U.S. and Ireland. To the delight of young actors, her scripts have vivid characterizations, vibrant dialogue, and liberal doses of comedy. Whether hilarious or serious and touching, they make grand audition and study pieces.

Jon Dorf's plays have been produced by such companies as InterAct, the Walnut Street Theatre, Moving Arts, the Pittsburgh New Works Festival and City Theater (Wilmington). Other venues for his work have included high schools, colleges, youth theatres, and even a military base. He has been a finalist in the Actors' Theatre of Louisville National Ten Minute Plays Contest, and is the former managing director and a life member of the Philadelphia Dramatists Center. He has taught playwriting at schools and theaters across the country, and he is a member of the Dramatists Guild and the Alliance of Los Angeles Playwrights.

Linda Eisenstein is an award-winning playwright, theatre composer, and poet whose nearly two dozen plays and musicals have been produced in the United States, Canada, Britain and Australia. Her plays have been published by Dramatic Publishing and appear in anthologies by Penguin, Heinemann, and Smith & Kraus. Her poetry and fiction have appeared in journals such as *Kalliope, The Cumberland Poetry Review, Kinesis,* and *Amelia.* A resident writer at the Cleveland Play House, she is a member of The Dramatists Guild, ASCAP, and the International Center for Women Playwrights.

Lynne Elson, a member of the Dramatists Guild, received the 2000 New York State Council on the Arts grant to create the community play CANCER'S NOT YOUR ONLY STORY. Her play MEMORY GLAND was semi-finalist at the Mill Mountain Theatre Festival. Her works have garnered critical acclaim from the *New York Times* and the *Off-Off-Broadway Review.* MEMORY GLAND had a successful run at the Women's Theatre Collective in New York City, and has received workshops at the Word of Mouth Reading Series, and the Pulse Ensemble. The monologues from MEMORY GLAND and BOONTOWN AND THE CINDERELLA COTTONBRAINS have been performed at The Actor's Institute, The Manhattan Theatre Source, and other various open mikes in Los Angeles, New York and New Jersey. She holds an M.F.A. from USC and teaches playwriting through Teachers and Writers Collaborative.

Philip Goulding was awarded an Arts Council of England Theatre Writing bursary in 1995 and has written for theatre, radio and television. His original stage plays are BENEATH THE WAVES (1993), THEN HE KISSED ME (1993), KID (1994), DIFFERENT ANIMAL (1995), WENT DOWN TO THE CROSSROADS (1997), WAITING FOR ELVIS (1998), TALL TALES FROM THE WEIRDWIDE WORLD (1999), and HEADING WEST (2000). His adaptations include ALICE IN WONDERLAND (1996), THE PIED PIPER (1997), THE GOVERNMENT INSPECTOR (1997), TOAD OF TOAD HALL (1998), THE MAYOR OF CASTERBRIDGE (1998), HANSEL AND GRETEL (1999), and PETER PAN (2000). Email: GouldingP@aol.com.

Lewis W. Heniford (b. April 16, 1928), M.L.S., Ph.D., teacher, actor, librarian, writer, studied at the University of North Carolina, Chapel Hill and at Stanford University. He has directed and produced over a thousand short plays in North Carolina, Montana, California, Germany and Mexico. Stanford Library stores the Lewis W. Heniford Collection, an archive of one-act plays.

Emilio Iasiello has received his M.F.A. from George Mason University. His poetry and short fiction have been published in numerous literary journals. He is the author of *Postcards from L.A.*, a chapbook of poems. His one-act plays have received several staged readings, and his one-act PAPIER-MACHE COWBOY was produced in New York in 2000. He is currently working on his first full-length play.

Rachel Rubin Ladutke is a New York-based playwright and director whose other works include CLARY'S EXODUS, LENNON, A LIFE and shorter pieces. GRACE NOTES and THE BELLES OF THE MILL have both been excerpted in numerous anthologies. GRACE NOTES received its premiere at the Gemini Theatre in Pittsburgh, as a winner of the 1999 Pittsburgh New Plays

Competition. Rachel is adapting THE BELLES OF THE MILL into both a musical and a screenplay. She is a member of the International Centre for Women Playwrights, and an Associate Member of The Dramatists Guild and SSDC.

Mary Lathrop's plays include HELL ON WHEELS, A BRIS IS STILL A BRIS, THE URN OF DREW, THE EIGHTEENTH MITZVAH and THE VISIBLE HORSE. Recent productions include DREAMS OF BABY at the Equity Library Theatre in Chicago, ONE MAGIC MOMENT at the HAGACTS '00 One Act Festival in Denver, and THE SIX BASIC RULES at Union Garage in Seattle. THE VISIBLE HORSE was workshopped at the 1996 Eugene O'Neill National Playwrights Conference, and first produced by the Whidby Island Center for the Arts in Langley, Washington.

David J. LeMaster received his Ph.D. from Texas Tech University and is a professor of Theatre and English at San Jacinto College in the Houston area. His publication credits include *Encore Performance Publishers, Original Works Publishing, Theatre Journal, This Month Onstage, The Journal of Popular Film and Television,* and *E-Always Entertainment.* Derald Mabbit holds a Masters degree from Texas Tech University. He and LeMaster have written a number of plays together, including a radio comedy of *Hamlet.*

Martha Lovely, Cathy Ryan, and **Katherine Burkman** all teach or have taught at the Ohio State University (Lovely in English, Ryan in the Business School, and Burkman in English, presently Professor Emerita). They are three of the ten members of WOMEN AT PLAY, whose other members are Lindsey Alexander, AnneMarie Brethauer, Jane Cottrell, Linda Meadows, Cecily O'Neill, Marilyn Rofsky, and Ann Roth. The group have been writing and performing their own dramas and those of others (Beckett and Pinter) since 1994, accompanied by guest artists, men as well as women. Among their original plays, produced in Columbus as site-specific events, are SHE FORGOT HER PURSE (1995), TALKING TO GLASS (1996), and IMAGINING IMOGENE (2000), Two other monologues from THE BLUEBERRY CAFE appear in Smith and Kraus' *Best Monologues of 1999.*

Bob Mayberry is co-founder of Attention Deficit Drama, a theatre group in West Michigan committed to short, experimental forms. Their most recent production was A MILLION MONOLOGUES FOR THE MILLENNIUM. Bob also teaches composition and playwriting at Grand Valley State University. His play DISAPPEARING IN NEPAL won the White Bird Annual Playwriting Contest in 1998. Other plays include WARM UP, ASSIGNATION, THE CATECHISM OF PATTY REED, EATING MEMORY, RAGTOWN, and THE THREE-MINUTE GODOT.

Scott McMorrow's award-winning plays have been produced both in Europe and the United States. His play, FISHING THE MOON, was a semifinalist in the Beverly Hills Theatre Guild Julie Harris Playwright Competition. His radio essays have aired on NPR affiliate KQED-FM. Additionally, he has published several books, magazine articles, and newspaper pieces.

Tim Miller has written about music, horses, ferrets, furniture and spiritual enlightenment for a growing number of publications and is perpetually at work on a book aimed at showing the interconnectedness of these and all other things. He lives on a farm in central Ohio with 19 horses and an undetermined number of dogs.

Sybil M. Odom, Ph.D., is a career educator and an internationally produced and published playwright. She is also a college professor and the founder of All Children' Theatre in Gainesville, Florida. She owes much to her muse and inspiration, Timothy Miller.

Gustavo Ott is a well-known Venezuelan author of short stories, essays, and scripts for stage and screen. He is also the founder and artistic director of the Teatro San Martin de Caracas, the city's major theatre for avant-garde work that has also toured its productions worldwide since 1996. Gustavo Ott's plays have been anthologized on several occasions, most recently in *Antologia Culpable* (1997) and *Las piezas que arrugan el corazon* (1998). His most well known plays include WHO EVER SAID I WAS A GOOD GIRL? (1995), FAT CHICKS (1993), PAVLOV (1997), and FOTOMATON. Gustavo Ott won the coveted Tirso de Molina prize in Spain in 1998, and has been the President of SARA (South American Regional Association) of the International Amateur Theatre Association since 1998.

Jamie Pachino is an award-winning playwright and screenwriter with national and international credits. Her plays have been produced in four countries, commissioned, published, and honored. In recent years, Jamie has been a winner of the Kennedy Center Fund for New American Plays production grant, twice nominated for the Osborn Award (American Theatre Critics Association), invited to the Women Playwrights Festival (ACT/Hedgebrook), and the Women's Playwriting Conference in Athens, Greece. Her plays THE RETURN TO MORALITY and AURORA'S MOTIVE have both been optioned for the screen, and her newest work, VISIBLE/INVISIBLE, was recently commissioned by Steppenwolf Theatre Company, Chicago.

Cary Pepper's work has been produced in Los Angeles, San Francisco and Edinburgh, among other cities. THE WALRUS SAID won the Religious Arts Guild Playwriting Competition, COME AGAIN, ANOTHER DAY was a winner in the San Francisco Playwrights Center "DramaRama '90" competition, and THE MALTESE FRENCHMAN was a finalist for the National Play Award. A screenwriter and novelist as well as a playwright, Cary is a member of the Dramatists Guild, and a founding member of the San Francisco theater groups ThroughLine and First Seen.

Sandra Perlman is an award-winning playwright and recipient of two Ohio Arts Council Playwriting Fellowships. A founding member of the Cleveland Play House Playwrights' Unit, some of her productions include: IN SEARCH OF RED RIVER DOG, COVERS, BEFORE THE WAR, NIGHT WALKING, DEAR MOTHER AND ALL, and UNIFORM LOVE. Her work has appeared in anthologies and literary journals and she has taught playwriting and creative writing seminars.

John Pinckard oversaw the creation and production of a number of original shows that were hailed for pushing the boundaries of youth theatre, while Artistic Director of All Children's Theatre. John holds a Bachelor's in theatre from the University of Florida and has taught acting and lighting design there and at several community colleges. He continues to write while pursuing an active career as an actor and director.

Lindsay Price divides her time between playwriting and her company, Theatrefolk. Most recently, her play EAT THE BREAST was workshopped by Famous Door Theatre in Chicago. This play also won the Theatre BC's 1998 National Playwriting Competition. Upcoming productions in 2001 include TUNA FISH EULOGY, FLASHBACKS, and THE FLYING BANDIT.

Lisa Rosenthal is a playwright, book author, and poet. Her work has been published and presented in the United States and has received numerous awards. Her plays include JUST THE SWEET STUFF (which contains the monolog in this collection), TENTH, NEIGHBORS, UNDER OUR CLOTHES, WELCOME TO MY NEIGHBORHOOD, CASEY AND EVELYN'S CHILD, and PERSONALLY YOURS.

Brian Torrey Scott has had two plays produced in recent years, including HISTRIONICA WITH BANJO at the New Visions, New Voices Festival in Dallas, and PICTURE OF A DOG at the Found Theatre in New York City. He has also made several films. He currently resides in Chicago.

Mark Wheeller's TOO MUCH PUNCH FOR JUDY (1988) is one of the most performed modern plays, with 4,500 performances between 1988 and 2000. Mark's plays have premiered at the Edinburgh Festival Fringe to great acclaim, and have been showcased at the National Student Drama Festival and the Lloyds Bank National Theatre Challenge at the Royal National Theatre in London. His most successful large cast musicals are THE MOST ABSURD XMAS MUSICAL IN THE WORLD ... EVER! (1998), and WACKY SOAP (2000).

Karin Diann Williams is Producing Director and Playwright-in-Residence at San Diego's Fritz Theater. Her plays have been produced and published internationally. The Fritz has staged her plays AUSTRALIA, ROOM, SUSAN KATRINA AND JILL, THE HATCHET, QUIZ, and THE THIRD VOICE OF THE NIGHTJAR. Her plays produced elsewhere include HEAD, SUNRISE, TEN O'CLOCK TUESDAY, and MEL IS A STRANGE GIRL. She earned her M.A. in Theatre from the University of New Mexico.

Christopher Woods lives in Texas. His plays have been produced in Chicago, Memphis, Minneapolis, Providence, Boston, Los Angeles and New York. He has published a novel, *The Dream Patch*. His prose collection, *Under a Riverbed Sky*, will be published in 2001. He teaches creative writing workshops in Houston.

Nancy Wright is an actor turned writer whose plays have been professionally produced in New York, Chicago, and Tampa. WHY COYOTES WON'T KILL YOU is about the aftermath of the Oklahoma City bombing: how one shattered individual finds the way back from hatred to hope. It was a finalist in the following competitions: The Marvin Taylor Playwriting Award, the Oglebay Institute Playwright's Award, the Siena International Playwriting Competition, and the Arlene R. and William P. Lewis Playwriting Contest at Brigham Young University.

Credits

BELLES OF THE MILL by Rachel Rubin Ladutke, © 1999 by Rachel Rubin Ladutke, all rights reserved. Reprinted by permission. Information concerning rights should be addressed to the author: Rachel Rubin Ladutke, webpage: www.geocities.com/darling1967. E-mail: darling67@theatermail.net. Tel.: 212.875.7785.

BOONTOWN AND THE CINDERELLA COTTONBRAINS by Lynne Elson. Copyright © 1994 by Lynne Elson. All rights reserved, including professional, amateur, public reading and reprints. Inquiries regarding rights should be addressed to the author at 534 East Freehold Road, Freehold NJ 07728.

THE CATECHISM OF PATTY REED by Bob Mayberry, © 2000 by Bob Mayberry, all rights reserved. Reprinted by permission. Information concerning rights should be addressed to the author: Bob Mayberry, E-mail: mayberrb@gvsu.edu.

DEAR MOTHER AND ALL by Sandra Perlman, © 2000 by Sandra Perlman, all rights reserved. Reprinted by permission. Information concerning rights should be addressed to the author: Sandra Perlman, P.O. Box 906, Kent, OH 44240. E-mail: www.sperlman.com.

DEVILS by Linda Eisenstein, © 1995 by Linda Eisenstein, all rights reserved. Reprinted by permission. Information concerning rights should be addressed to the author: Linda Eisenstein, P.O. Box 749, Cleveland, OH 44107-0749, E-mail: herone@en.com.

DUCK BLIND by Shirley Barrie, © 2000 by Shirley Barrie, all rights reserved. Reprinted by permission. Information concerning rights should be addressed to the Playwrights Union of Canada, 54 Wolseley St., 2nd floor, Toronto, Ontario M5T 1A5. E-mail: cdplays@interlog.com.

EMBALMING by Karin Diann Williams, copyright © 1999 by Karin Diann Williams. All rights reserved. Reprinted by permission of the author. Inquiries regarding rights should be addressed to the author at P.O. Box 127778, San Diego CA 92112-7778, E-mail: karindiann@mindspring.com.

FISHING THE MOON by Scott McMorrow, copyright © 1999 by Scott McMorrow. All rights reserved. Reprinted by permission of the author. Inquiries regarding rights should be addressed to the author at 1111 Greenwood Avenue, Palo Alto CA 94301, E-mail: www.scottmcmorrow.com.

FIVE DAYS TO FRIDAY by John Pinckard, copyright © 1999 by John Pinckard. All rights reserved. Reprinted by permission of the author. Inquiries regarding rights should be addressed to the author at P.O. Box 53, Ruskin, FL 33570, E-mail: jlpinck@hotmail.com.

FUN HOUSE MIRROR by Dori Appel, © 1999 by Dori Appel, all rights reserved.

THE GOVERNMENT INSPECTOR by Nickolai Gogol, in a version by Philip Goulding. © 1998 by Philip Goulding. All rights are strictly reserved and application for performance etc., must be made before the start of any rehearsal to the author's agent: Eric Glass Ltd., 28 Berkeley Square, London W1X 6HD, UNITED KINGDOM. E-mail: Eglassltd@aol.com.

GRACE NOTES by Rachel Rubin Ladutke, © 1998 by Rachel Rubin Ladutke, all rights reserved. Reprinted by permission. Information concerning rights should be addressed to the author: Rachel Rubin Ladutke, web page www.geocities.com/darling1967, E-mail darling67@theatermail.net, Telephone 212.875.7785.

HEADING WEST by Philip Goulding, © 2000 by Philip Goulding. All rights are strictly reserved and application for performance etc., must be made before the start of any rehearsal to the author's agent: Eric Glass Ltd., 28 Berkeley Square, London W1X 6HD, UNITED KINGDOM. E-mail: Eglassltd@aol.com.

HISTRIONICA WITH BANJO by Brian Torrey Scott, © 1998 by Brian Torrey Scott, all rights reserved. Reprinted by permission. Information concerning rights should be addressed to the author at 7116 Nicki Court., Dallas TX 75252, E-mail: briantorrey@go.com.

I AM MARGUERITE by Shirley Barrie, © 2000 by Shirley Barrie, all rights reserved. Reprinted by permission. Information concerning rights should be addressed to the Playwrights Union of Canada, 54 Wolseley St., 2nd floor, Toronto, Ontario M5T 1A5. E-mail: cdplays@interlog.com.

THE LESSON by Lisa Rosenthal, © 2000 by Lisa Rosenthal. All rights reserved. Reprinted by permission of the author. Inquiries regarding rights should be addressed to the author at 7363 N. Seeley Avenue #3N, Chicago IL 60645.

A LIST FOR REB PINCHAS by Sandra Fenichel Asher. Copyright © 2000 by Sandra Fenichel Asher. All rights reserved. Send monolog inquiries to the author at 721 South Weller Avenue, Springfield, MO 65802, E-mail: sasher@lib.drury.edu. *A LIST FOR REB PINCHAS* is adapted from *THE WISE MEN OF CHELM* by Sandra Fenichel Asher. Copyright © 1992 by Sandra Fenichel Asher. Inquiries about the full script should be addressed to Dramatic Publishing Company, 311 Washington Street, Woodstock IL 60098, 1-800-HIT-SHOW, E-mail: plays@dramaticpublishing.com.

LISTEN TO OUR VOICES by Claire Braz-Valentine, © 2000 by Claire Braz-Valentine. All rights reserved. Reprinted by permission of the author. Inquiries

addressed to Sybil M. Odom, 1707 SW 56th Lane, Gainseville FL 32608. E-mail: SybilOdom@aol.com.

PRESSURE by Lindsay Price, copyright © 1999 by Lindsay Price, all rights reserved. Reprinted by permission of the author. Inquiries regarding rights should be addressed to the author at 2873 Dundas Street West, Suite 302, Toronto, Ontario, CANADA M6P 1Y9, E-mail: www.theatrefolk.com.

THE SISTER by Timothy Miller, copyright © 2000 by Timothy Miller, all rights reserved. Reprinted by permission of the author. Inquiries regarding rights should be addressed to the author: Timothy Miller, Rocky Point Farm, 3746 Old Mill Road, Springfield, OH, 45502.

SISTERS OF SISTERS by Cynthia L. Cooper, © 2000 by Cynthia L. Cooper, all rights reserved. Excerpt entitled *The Note* is reprinted by permission. Information concerning rights should be addressed to the author: Cynthia L. Cooper, 446 W. 47th Street, #1-B, New York NY 10036, E-mail: coopcyn@mindspring.com.

THIS PHONE WILL EXPLODE AT THE TONE by Lindsay Price, copyright © 2000 by Lindsay Price, all rights reserved. Reprinted by permission of the author. Inquiries regarding rights should be addressed to the author at 2873 Dundas Street West, Suite 302, Toronto, Ontario, CANADA M6P 1Y9, E-mail: www.theatrefolk.com.

TOO MUCH PUNCH FOR JUDY by Mark Wheeller, copyright © 1987 and 1999 by Mark Wheeller, all rights reserved. Reprinted by permission of the author. Inquiries regarding rights should be addressed to the author's agent: at MBA Literary Agents Ltd., 62 Grafton Way, London W1P 5LD, United Kingdom. E-mail: Meg@mbalit.co.uk.

UNDER THE BIG TOP by Emilio Iasiello, © 2000 by Emilio Iasiello, all rights reserved. Reprinted by permission. Information concerning rights should be addressed to the author: Emilio Iasiello, 2428 13th Court North, Arlington, VA 22209, E-mail: IasielloEJ@state.gov.

THE VISIBLE HORSE by Mary Lathrop, © 2000 by Mary Lathrop. CAUTION. All rights reserved. Reprinted with permission of the AUTHOR. Professionals and amateurs are hereby warned that *THE VISIBLE HORSE* is subject to a royalty. It is fully protected under the copyright laws of the United States, and all countries covered by the International Copyright Union and/or the Pan-American Copyright Convention and/or all countries with which the United States has reciprocal copyright relations. All rights, without exception, are strictly reserved. Inquiries should be made to the Author: Mary Lathrop, 116 Raye Street, Seattle WA 98109. 206.285.7244. E-mail: lathrop@sprynet.com.

should be addressed to the author: Nancy Wright, Laughing Moon Ponds, 12385 Horton Road, Riga, MI 49276-9794.

About the Editor

Roger Ellis earned his M.A. in English and Drama from the University of Santa Clara, and his Ph.D. in Dramatic Art from the University of California at Berkeley. During that time he was also guest stage director for several colleges and universities. He has authored or edited ten books in theatre, plus numerous articles, essays and short stories. In 1991 he initiated an ethnic theatre program at Grand Valley State University in Michigan, creating guest artist residencies and staging plays celebrating cultural diversity; and he has been director of the University's Shakespeare Festival since 1993. He has worked professionally as actor or director with various Michigan and California theatres; and has served as President of the Theatre Alliance of Michigan for the past six years. He often serves as an adjudicator for high school forensics and thespian activities; as well as for stage productions in the United States and internationally. He frequently conducts workshops in acting and auditioning skills for theatres in the United States and abroad. He is currently a Professor of Theatre at Grand Valley State University.